THE
POPULATION
OF THE UK

For Alison Rachel Dorling

2ND Edition

THE
POPULATION
OF THE UK

DANIEL DORLING

with cartography by **Benjamin D. Hennig**

Los Angeles | London | New Delhi
Singapore | Washington DC

Los Angeles | London | New Delhi
Singapore | Washington DC

SAGE Publications Ltd
1 Oliver's Yard
55 City Road
London EC1Y 1SP

SAGE Publications Inc.
2455 Teller Road
Thousand Oaks, California 91320

SAGE Publications India Pvt Ltd
B 1/I 1 Mohan Cooperative Industrial Area
Mathura Road
New Delhi 110 044

SAGE Publications Asia-Pacific Pte Ltd
3 Church Street
#10-04 Samsung Hub
Singapore 049483

Editor: Robert Rojek
Editorial assistant: Alana Clogan
Production editor: Katherine Haw
Copyeditor: Solveig Gardner Servian
Proofreader: H. A. Fairlie
Indexer: Judith Lavender
Marketing manager: Michael Ainsley
Cover design: Francis Kenney
Typeset by: C&M Digitals (P) Ltd, Chennai, India
Printed in India at Replika Press Pvt Ltd

© Daniel Dorling 2013

First edition published 2005 as *Human Geography of the UK*

This edition first published 2013

Library of Congress Control Number: 2012935336

British Library Cataloguing in Publication data

A catalogue record for this book is available from
the British Library

ISBN 978–1–4462–5296–3
ISBN 978–1–4462–5297–0 (pbk)

The cover image, being taken from a work of art,
obviously excludes parts of Ireland, the Shetland Isles
and other areas outside of mainland UK.

Contents

List of figures and tables

Figures

Tables

About the author

Danny Dorling is a Professor of Human Geography at the University of Sheffield. With a group of colleagues he helped create the website www.worldmapper.org which shows who has most and least in the world. He has published with others more than 30 books on issues related to social inequalities and several hundred journal papers. Much of this work is available by open access (see www.dannydorling. org). His work concerns issues of housing, health, employment, education and poverty. His recent books include three co-authored texts: *Identity in Britain: A cradle-to-grave atlas*; *The Atlas of the Real World: Mapping the way we live*; and *Bankrupt Britain: An atlas of social change*. Recent sole authored books include *Injustice: Why social inequalities persist* in 2010; *So You Think You Know about Britain* and *Fair Play*, both in 2011; and the *No Nonsense Guide to Equality* in 2012.

He has been a member of the World Health Organization's Scientific Resource Group on Health Equity Analysis and Research. He is a Patron of the charity RoadPeace, an Academician of the Academy of the Learned Societies in the Social Sciences and, in 2008, became Honorary President of the Society of Cartographers.

Before a career in academia Danny was employed as a play-worker in children's play-schemes and in pre-school education where the underlying rationale was that playing is learning for living. This might explain some of the more unusual material that is in the book.

Preface

This book has been written for students at university studying at the start of the second decade of the twenty-first century, assumed to be living in, or interested in, the UK. The population of these countries is presented here in a way that is unusual in contemporary teaching.

First, the population is mainly described through maps, and the maps in this book are based on a new and very novel projection. Although they initially appear to be showing a crude landscape of the UK, the shape of areas on the maps shows a social rather than a physical landscape. Areas are drawn in size in proportion to the numbers of people being depicted. This, after all, is a book about the population of the UK.

Second, this book uses quantitative evidence. Trends from the 1990s, from around the millennium, and more recent birth and death statistics have been brought together to draw the maps and figures shown here. In all cases sources and methods are given, in many cases in sufficient detail to allow a student to replicate these illustrations through simply having access to the Internet.

Third, this book is not written as an objective account, although the use of quantitative evidence can give that impression. Instead, the book is a story of some of the aspects of life in the UK which are most influenced by people's times, places and ages, and a story that begins with ways of imagining childhood and education. It is a story about things that interest me and which I think affect most people, thus issues of identity, ideology and inequality appear at the heart of the book. It ends where it began: with a view of children's lives, but a view of how the children of the UK fit within a global picture of human geography. This is necessarily a partial, parochial, and particular story of the population of these countries.

What this book does hopefully achieve is, at the very least, a description of the UK which is different from most that have been presented before. This book is based on an earlier text, *Human Geography of the UK*, which has now been revised to look back from the vantage point of 2012 on what was thought to be going on a few years ago. All the maps and graphics have been both redesigned and redrawn in full colour for this edition. Previously missing data for Northern Ireland, on births in the last decades, deaths in the last year, student numbers and the 2005 and 2010 general elections have all been added, and most of what was shown before is now interpreted a little differently to how it looked seven years ago.

This book provides a description painted from numbers collected to record key moments in people's lives: their births, movements, literacy, exam results, how they are labelled by the state, how their voices are counted within its democracy, their incomes, expenditures, work, caring, deaths, homes and how these appear when contrasted with the narrow global context of worldwide childhood poverty (Chapter 10). The text accompanying these descriptions suggests something of the processes that have created these images.

For anyone using this book in teaching about the UK, the figures have all been made available as PowerPoint slides on an accompanying website. (See link on this page: http://www.dannydorling.org/). At the end of each chapter a possible activity is described whereby students can themselves carry out an exercise which illustrates part of what is being suggested in the chapter. Just as you often learn far more by looking at source data than by reading other people's summaries of it, so too it is better to play out what is being described rather than simply listen to such a description in a lecture.

All the exercises given at the end of each chapter are ones that I have used in teaching students ranging (now) from age 8 to 80, with between 12 and 270 in a group. It should not be difficult to interest students in the population of a country, especially if they form a part of that population, but somehow we often manage to turn what should be the most interesting and directly relevant of subjects into an academic exercise in passing exams.

The human geography, economics, politics, demography and sociology of the UK is not only of interest to those whose bodies help make it up, those who can expect to play out most of the remainder of their lives in it. It is also of interest to many people living outside the UK. England, Scotland, Wales and Northern Ireland are a very rich set of countries, as is made abundantly evident in the final chapter of the book. The key question to ask throughout this book is why, given the resources that we have, do we organise ourselves across these countries in this way? Why do we most often have children where we do at the ages that we do? Why do we sort children out both through space and education as shown here? Why do we label people as we do? Why are most of their votes wasted (if they use them)? Why do so many live in poverty? Why can so many not read and write in such rich countries?

Why do we tolerate inequalities in illness and death which are so clear to see in the maps shown here? Why have we allowed what were our most successful industries to continue to become as geographically concentrated as they have? What really made them appear successful, and why are we still migrating towards those (financial) industries so that many of us are squeezed into very little space, while others watch their areas empty out? But before you can ask why, you need to know what has happened, to whom, when, and where. You need to start with the population of the UK.

Acknowledgements

All faults in the approach, text, figures and statistics presented in this book lie with me. I am most grateful to Ben Hennig for agreeing to undertake the cartographic work needed to produce the maps shown here, which was well beyond my abilities. In this he was assisted by Graham Allsopp and Paul Coles, cartographers at the University of Sheffield, to whom thanks are also due.

JJan Rigby, Dimitris Ballas, Bronwen and David Dorling commented on various drafts of the original manuscript, helped turn my elementary English into something a little more readable and to tone down my more bizarre suggestions. I am particularly grateful to Jan for her ability to spot numerous inadvertent *double entendres* and *faux pas*. Any remaining are obviously ones she enjoyed too much to bring to my attention.

Robert Rojek and Sophie Hine of SAGE Publications helped coax this edition into life and were very encouraging throughout the rewriting, including soliciting a series of reviews of the first book to help in its revision. I am grateful to all those anonymous reviewers, especially the undergraduates and whoever had the idea of asking them. The original idea for a book of this kind should also be accredited to Robert; I hope I have repaid that work a little in that this edition is at least not as delayed as was the first. Solveig Gardner Servian did a brilliant job of copyediting the text and Katherine Haw was exceptionally efficient in seeing through its production. I am also grateful to Helen Fairlie for careful final proof reading.

I am grateful to my colleagues at the universities of Bristol, Leeds and Sheffield for their support when I first, and later, taught on some of the subjects in these pages, to many of the geography students of those institutions in recent years who kindly endured my experiments in trying to learn how to become a lecturer, and to friends at many conferences and meetings over the last few years who commented on many of the ideas and images that have now found their way into these pages.

Finally, I must express my gratitude to the various companies that took over upon the privatisation of British Rail. The excellent way in which they have run the train network of the UK since then was largely responsible for giving me the often unplanned time to contemplate what kind of human geography made up these countries. In recent years that contemplative service improved greatly. After all, what else is there to think about when staring out of a window wondering exactly where you are, who lives in those houses, how they ended up living there, what they do, just how crowded can this train get, why don't they ever add the extra carriages that were promised, and when you might be moving again.

Danny Dorling, somewhere near Trent Junction (again!)

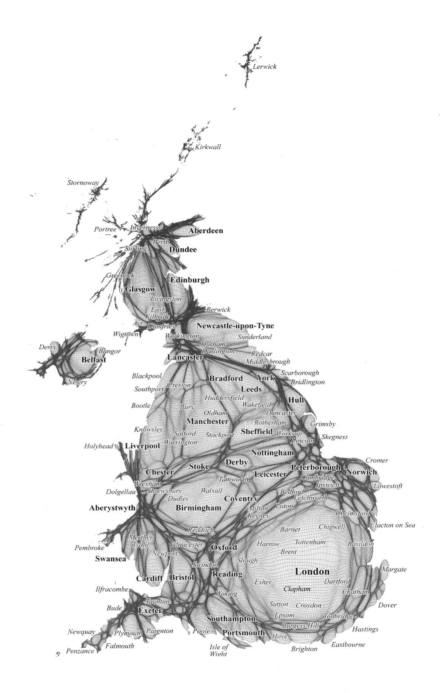

Enlarged inset of the labelled cartogram in Figure 1.2 (page 4)

1

MAPS

... a different view of the UK

This chapter suggests that your view of these countries has been created by the environment in which you grew up. Throughout this book the reader is assumed to be an 18-year-old student who has just gone to university or is just about to go there. Your view of the UK has been built up through how the media have depicted the UK, through how you were taught at school to view human geography, and through what your friends and family told you.

If you grew up in Britain then you grew up with the view shown on the right of Figure 1.1. However, throughout this book the view on the left will be used (see page xiv overleaf). Both images show the same value at every place – the height of land. But the gridded population cartogram on the left uses a map projection that gives every person equal space and shows that most people live at relatively low heights (at low altitude). The land-area map on the right is good for studying land. It is the traditional map used by the media in Britain, but it is not a good map to use to see people.

The media need to sell newspapers or gain viewers and listeners. They tend to present a salacious view of life in Britain, concentrating on the highs and lows, on the lives of the very rich and the travails of the very poor. Ultimately the media consist of just another collection of people, most of whom were very like you when they were 18. What they were taught and how they were shown the country and world they lived in influenced them too.

One thing you can be sure of is that the picture of the UK presented in this short book is not the picture that was presented a decade or two ago. However, this book too is just as influenced by its author's exposure to the media, the schools he attended, and the views of his family and friends as your views are. I've just had a little more time to think about these things, and I think we can look at these countries in a new way as a result of those influences and that thinking. What I am asking you to do is to bear with me while I try to present you with a different view of the country you grew up in. I am trying to present that view from your point of view. This chapter begins by looking at where 18-year-olds live, and which of them go to university. How uneven is this landscape, and how in turn is that likely to be shaping the view of the UK which university students have?

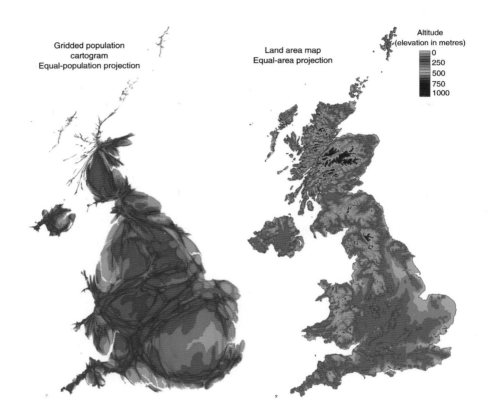

Figure 1.1 Topography: gridded UK population cartogram and UK land area map

Note: The cartogram gives every person the same amount of space. Each faintly drawn grid cell on the cartogram relates to the same amount of space in the physical world. The size of a grid cell reflects the number of people living in that space in relation to the other grid cells.

Source: Population: SEDAC Columbia University (2010); Topography: US Geological Survey (2011).

We begin with a question: From where are you looking at the UK? To start to answer that question we need a simple picture of the UK. The new map used here is one that has never been drawn in any book before. Throughout this book just 85 areas on it will be shaded, but despite this simplicity the new map can be used to unveil a great deal about the human geography of these countries, its people and, first, its 18-year-olds.

You are used to a particular map of the UK. This is the map you grew up with, the one used in most textbooks and which appears on television every evening in the weather reports, the map which shows the UK as it appears from space. However, looking at the UK from space is not the best way to see its population. More people live in London than Scotland, for instance.

The alternative map of the UK, shown with places labelled on it on the left of Figure 1.2, presents a picture which tries to give the people of the UK fairer representation and allows us to see upon it variations within large cities alongside variations between regions and between more rural areas simultaneously. Grid lines are shown drawn faintly on the cartogram; they depict areas of the same size when drawn on a land-area map, but here every 'square' has its area made proportional to its population.

The grid lines in Figure 1.2 coalesce in sparsely populated rural areas. The grid is not shown on the ordinary land area map in Figure 1.1 because its lines would all be too close together to see any individual squares. An ordinary map would have to be thousands of times bigger to show much of the detail about people's lives that the cartogram shows, and it would still distort things from the perspective of most of the population. However, the grid is shown on all of the cartogram-maps that follow to remind you that these are not just diagrams, but maps of real places with the topology (areas that touch each other) preserved.

On the map on the right of Figure 1.2 are shown the 85 constituencies drawn up in 1999 for the European parliamentary elections of that year. Northern Ireland was defined as one large constituency that would return three members of the parliament. At the last minute the UK government chose a different voting system for that election and so these areas were not used in that election. We use them here as they present a way of grouping the population of the UK into large adjacent areas, each containing roughly the same number of people.

While you may not be used to the map shown in Figure 1.2, the names of the areas on that map listed in Table 1.1 should be a little more familiar. These are the labels for the 85 constituencies used in the rest of this book. Most are named after old counties or parts of counties. They were designed to each contain roughly half a million electors (people aged 18 or over) and to combine together those electors who had most in common geographically.

Note these maps are identical to the fold out maps at the end of this book which have been included to allow you to locate places easily without having to turn back to pages 4 and 5 continuously.

Use the list of names in Table 1.1 and the two maps in Figure 1.2 to identify in which constituencies you have lived. If you have difficulty doing this, the full list of which areas make up each constituency is given in the Appendix at the end of this book. Once you have identified your constituency you can see where, on this new map of the UK, you have lived.

Figure 1.1 shows not only each area of the UK drawn roughly in proportion to the size of its population, but also the underlying physical landscape (topography). It also shows the map drawn using a conventional equal-area projection. The disadvantage of using a conventional map is that those areas that are home to most people are obscured in comparison to sparsely populated places which appear most prominent. The advantage of showing a physical topography on both these maps is that it shows that even aspects of

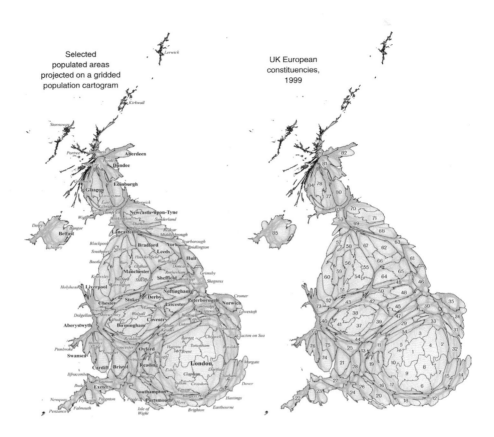

Figure 1.2 Selected population areas and UK European constituencies in 1999

Source: UK European Constituencies obtained from the House of Commons Research Paper 98/102. See Table 1.1, opposite, for the constituency key and page xiv for an enlarged inset of the labelled cartogram.

physical geography can be displayed on a population projection and tell us something new (in this case the altitudes at which people live).

Topography is a familiar depiction: rivers run down mountains; temperature tends to fall as the land rises. In human geography there is no single obvious variable to use to map the basic contours of the social landscape. In the first edition of this book the height on all the maps was drawn in proportion to a child's chances of winning a place to attend university. The result was a little confusing, so here a more detailed but flat equal-population cartogram projection is used. The projection and all the maps included here were created by Ben Hennig (see www.viewsoftheworld.net).

The new map has been created to provide a fairer base to look at the life of a hypothetical university student who turned 18 in the year 2000, and hence (with luck) 30 in the year 2012. Where might that student have come from? Figure 1.3 provides an answer based on how many 15-year-olds attended

Table 1.1   Areas that never existed – UK European constituencies, 1999

London

1   London Central
2   London East
3   London North
4   London North East
5   London North West
6   London South and Surrey East
7   London South East
8   London South Inner
9   London South West
10 London West

South East

11 Buckinghamshire and Oxfordshire East
12 East Sussex and Kent South
13 Hampshire North and Oxford
14 Kent East
15 Kent West
16 South Downs West
17 Surrey
18 Sussex West
19 Thames Valley
20 Wight and Hampshire South

South West

21 Bristol
22 Cornwall and West Plymouth
23 Devon and East Plymouth
24 Dorset and East Devon
25 Gloucestershire
26 Itchen, Test and Avon
27 Somerset and North Devon
28 Wiltshire North and Bath

East of England

29 Bedfordshire and Milton Keynes
30 Cambridgeshire
31 Essex North and Suffolk South
32 Essex South
33 Essex West and Hertfordshire East
34 Hertfordshire
35 Norfolk
36 Suffolk and South West Norfolk

West Midlands

37 Birmingham East
38 Birmingham West
39 Coventry and North Warwickshire
40 Herefordshire and Shropshire
41 Midlands West
42 Staffordshire East and Derby
43 Staffordshire West and Congleton
44 Worcestershire and South Warwickshire

East Midlands

45 Leicester
46 Lincolnshire
47 Northamptonshire and Blaby
48 Nottingham and Leicestershire North West
49 Nottinghamshire North and Chesterfield
50 Peak District

North West

51 Cheshire East
52 Cheshire West and Wirral
53 Cumbria and Lancashire North
54 Greater Manchester Central
55 Greater Manchester East
56 Greater Manchester West
57 Lancashire Central
58 Lancashire South
59 Merseyside East and Wigan
60 Merseyside West

Yorkshire and the Humber

61 East Yorkshire and North Lincolnshire
62 Leeds
63 North Yorkshire
64 Sheffield
65 Yorkshire South
66 Yorkshire South West
67 Yorkshire West

North East

68 Cleveland and Richmond
69 Durham
70 Northumbria
71 Tyne and Wear

Wales

72 Mid and West Wales
73 North Wales
74 South Wales Central
75 South Wales East
76 South Wales West

Scotland

77 Central Scotland
78 Glasgow
79 Highlands and Islands
80 Lothian
81 Mid Scotland and Fife
82 North East Scotland
83 South of Scotland
84 West of Scotland

Northern Ireland

85 Ulster (Northern Ireland)

Source: House of Commons Research Paper 98/102 (map on page 49). Available at www.parliament.
uk/commons/lib/research/rp98/rp98-102.pdf.

schools in each constituency three years earlier. The Figure records, to the nearest thousand, the number of people within each European constituency area who turned 18 in the year 2000.

Figure 1.3   People aged 18 in 2000

Note: Counts by European Constituency area.

Source: Estimated from school rolls of 15-year-olds in 1997 and 2000 mid-year estimate for Northern Ireland.

Figure 1.3 shows disparities of the order of many thousands in the number of people who turned 18 in each area of Britain in 2000. Part of the pattern will be due to the fact that each constituency was designed to contain roughly half a million voters, not exactly equal numbers of people (there were just over a million voters in the three Northern Ireland seats). To see the degree to which there is actual variation in this population group we need to divide the numbers counted for Figure 1.3 by the total population living in each constituency.

Actual variation can be ascertained by calculating rates. Figure 1.4 shows the 18-year-olds as a proportion of the total population living in each constituency, by where they were at school when aged 15. The pattern it shows is of low proportions of 18-year-olds living around the south coast, in London and in the centres of some other large cities. The three areas with the lowest proportions were London South Inner, London Central and London South West, followed by Sheffield. What led to less than 1% of the population being aged 18 in these places?

Figure 1.4 Proportion aged 18 in 2000

Source: Estimated from school rolls of 15-year-olds in 1997 and mid-year population estimates for 2000.

Eighteen-year-olds are most likely to come from the more suburban and rural constituencies of the UK. The highest proportions are found in Lancashire South, followed by the West, Centre and Highlands of Scotland then by Cheshire East, Cleveland & Richmond (North Yorkshire) and Yorkshire West. By the time their children are aged 15, a significant proportion of parents have moved their family homes away from the city centres. Later we'll see how many were born in cities and more about this selective migration.

Table 1.2 The two extreme European constituencies compared

London North West	UCAS	School	%	Yorkshire South	UCAS	School	%
Harrow East	765	1142	67%	Don Valley	280	1105	25%
Brent East	360	541	67%	Rotherham	215	897	24%
Brent North	590	978	60%	Doncaster Central	250	1165	21%
Hayes & Harlington	265	499	53%	Doncaster North	165	802	21%
Brent South	400	790	51%	Barnsley Central	155	1031	15%
Harrow West	650	1340	49%	Wentworth	185	1324	14%
				Barnsley East and			
Ruislip-Northwood	400	956	42%	Mexborough	165	1396	12%
Uxbridge	280	1156	24%	Rother Valley	140	1240	11%
Total	3710	7402	50%	Total	1555	8960	17%

Note: UCAS = successful applicants; School = number of pupils aged 15.

Source: Estimated from school rolls of 15 year olds in 1997 and mid-year population estimates for 2000.

One reason for the drift of children to the suburbs could perhaps be that some parents are attempting to improve their offspring's life chances by moving house (or flat). For the cohort born in 1982, Figure 1.5 shows the proportion of 18-year-olds who entered higher education from each constituency. It ranges from one-sixth (17%) to half (50%). Although entry from much of Scotland and North Wales is above average, in general higher proportions enter from the suburban and southern constituencies. However, the children with the highest chances of going to university went to school in a city constituency: London North West (50.1% entry), closely followed by more rural Surrey (47.7%).

The constituency where children's chance of going to university was lowest was Yorkshire South (17.4%), where children were almost three times less likely to go to university than in London North West. It is worth noting that the estimate for Northern Ireland is almost certainly an underestimate as it does not include participation of students from Northern Ireland in universities in the Republic of Ireland. What was your chance of going to university? Note that since these statistics were collected most people's chances will have risen, although application to universities in the UK fell in late 2011 as higher fees were announced.

Statistics about people should never be taken at face value. Table 1.2 shows the numbers that were used to calculate the statistics for the most extreme two areas shown in Figure 1.5. The European constituencies of both London North West and Yorkshire South were defined as a combination of eight (1997) UK parliamentary constituencies (see Appendix). Within each European constituency there is a great deal of geographical variation. For instance, taking the extreme two parliamentary constituencies you could claim that children in Harrow East were six times more likely to go to university than children growing up in the Rother Valley. If you wanted to downplay the differences, you could point out that children in Uxbridge were less likely to go to university than children in the Don Valley. But how reliable are these figures?

Although there may have been 1,156 children aged 15 attending schools in Uxbridge in 1997, more of those children probably lived outside that parliamentary constituency than commuted out of it to go to school. The Universities & Colleges Admissions Service (UCAS) figures for entry to university are based on people's home address, not their school's address. We are therefore not strictly comparing like with like, and this is before we start to worry about the migration of children between age 15 and when they apply to university. At the level of the European constituencies such problems are less acute because a far lower proportion of children will cross European constituency boundaries to go to school. Nevertheless, for the data that is presented to you as fact, it always pays to think about where it comes from.

Figure 1.5   Proportion of 18-year-olds going to university in 2000

Source: Successful UCAS under age 21 applicants from National Statistics website and estimated for Scotland and Northern Ireland.

The UCAS data that has been used so far in this chapter is provided on the government's official website for every local government ward in England (www. neighbourhood.statistics.gov.uk). If we knew a reliable count of the population eligible to apply to university from each ward, we could produce statistics that showed even starker geographical differences than those presented so far.

If statistics within one country are difficult to interpret, check and understand, the statistics that compare rates between countries are even more problematic. Figure 1.6 presents participation rates for this cohort when in secondary education for 14 Western European countries. The rate for the UK (highlighted, at 32%) was very low in comparison with most other countries and surprisingly similar to the rate entering universities some four years after this data was collected. Note that this is the 'full-time' participation rate and note when the data was collected.

A large part of the reason for the overall level of university entry in the UK having been low in the recent past was due to a traditionally low level of staying on at school past the compulsory age of 16 (it is rising soon). For instance, in Belgium, the Netherlands and Germany the school leaving age has been 18 for many years. When trying to estimate a child's chances of going to university what matters most is that they grew up in an affluent area like the UK, but one which traditionally has had low participation at age 18. The next most

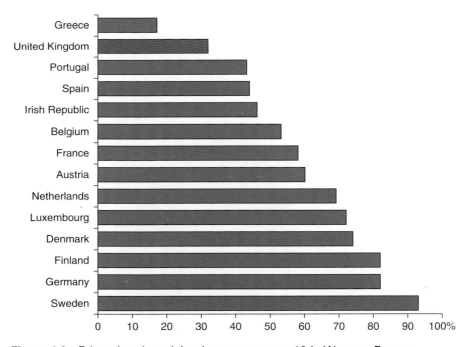

Figure 1.6 Educational participation rates at age 18 in Western Europe

Note: UK highlighted; data for Italy was missing.

Source: Full-time participation in secondary education at age 18 in 1996, *Social Trends 30*.

important factor after that is also geographical: where they grew up within the UK, as rates vary so much by area.

How do we know that location is so important in determining an 18-year-old's chances of going to university? Surely it could just be that children growing up in better-off families are more likely to go and those families are concentrated in particular places? Well, the advantage of counting these things is that we can check these ideas.

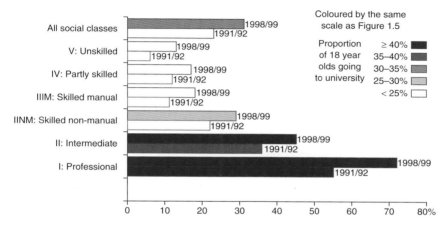

Figure 1.7   People under 21 attending university by social class

Note: The six social classes shown above are based on the occupations of the parents of those young adults whose chances are being depicted.

Source: Social Trends 30, data from the National Statistics website (for GB).

Figure 1.7 shows the increasing proportions of students attending university according to the occupations of their parents. The distribution is very uneven, became more uneven during the 1990s, but it (not shown with this data) had become slightly more equitable by 2010. Back at the turn of the millennium, 72% of the children of parents in professional occupations were going to university as compared to 13% of the children of parents in occupations labelled as unskilled. The graph is coloured by the same shades as were used in Figure 1.5. Looking at this graph you might be led to believe that it was these differences that account for the geography of participation shown in Figure 1.5 earlier. How do we go about checking that?

For each European constituency we know the proportion of children (aged 0–15) of parents of different occupations as recorded in the 1991 census. Those children had an average age of between 7 and 8 in 1991 and so are roughly representative of our 18-year-old adults in 2000 – those who are in their early thirties now. The social profile of areas also tends to change only slowly over time. Areas with lots of people in professional occupations in one year tend to have lots of people in those occupations in the next year. Thus the social profile of children by area by the class of their parents can be expected to have been fairly constant since 1991.

So, given that we know the proportion of children in each social class in each area and the proportion of children from each social class who go to university, what would we expect the proportion of children going to universities from any given area to be?

For our two extreme constituencies Table 1.3 presents the proportions of children in each social class using the same labels as in Figure 1.7. More than twice as many 1990s children had parents in social class I (professional) in London North West (9%) when compared to Yorkshire South (4%). More than twice as many children in Yorkshire South (7%) had parents in unskilled occupations as in London North West (3%). The two constituencies look to have had very different social profiles. In a way they did, at the extremes, but in each roughly three-quarters of all children have parents in social classes II, IIINM and IIIM (combined). How might these differing constituency social profiles be expected to result in differing numbers of children going to university from these two places?

The mathematics for a prediction can be very simple. Here we just take the national proportion of children going to university in each social class and multiply that by the proportion of children in that class in each place to produce a prediction of what proportion of children of each class in each place we would expect to have gone to university in the last decade. Thus we would expect 72% of the 9% of children in social class I in London North West to have gone to university: 72% of 9% = 7%. Summing the predicted proportions for London North West suggests that 33% of children there should have gone to university. Doing the same for Yorkshire South suggests 27% should have gone if class alone determined a child's future.

We know that the actual proportions of 18-year-olds going to university from the two extreme constituencies was 50% and 17%, which were 17% higher and 10% lower than we might predict. To put it another way, allowing for the differing social class profiles of these areas only helps to explain 6% (33% − 27%) of the 33% (50% − 17%) variation between them, or about

Table 1.3 Children by social class and predicted university entry rates (percentages)

Children by social class	I	II	IIINM	IIIM	IV	V	Total
London North West	9	34	14	30	9	3	100
Yorkshire South	4	22	9	41	18	7	100
GB % going to University	72	45	29	18	17	13	31
Predicted proportions							
London North West	7	15	4	5	2	0	33
Yorkshire South	3	10	3	7	3	1	27
Actual proportions							
London North West							50
Yorkshire South							17

Source: 1991 Census 10% statistics and *Social Trends 30*, data from the National Statistics website (for GB), 1998/99 (for class labels). NM = Non Manual, M = Manual.

one-sixth of the geographical variation. Although there are very great differences in university entry rates between the chances of children whose parents have different occupations, the distribution of children by social class does not vary that greatly geographically. At least it does not vary that greatly between these areas, which each contain roughly half a million electors. Each of these large areas has its share of children from better-off and worse-off families. For the places where most and least go to university, the differing social profiles of these areas only explain a minor part of the differing levels of university entrance.

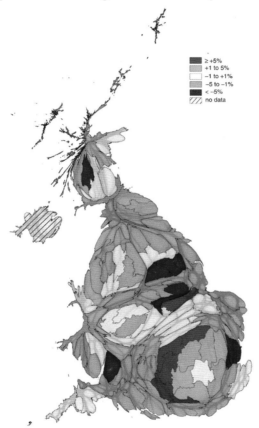

Figure 1.8 Differences between observed and expected university entry rates allowing for the geography of children's social class

Note: Northern Ireland is excluded as no comparable census data was available.

Source: Successful UCCAs under age 21 applicants from National Statistics website.

Figure 1.8 presents the results of subtracting the proportion of children we might have expected to have gone to university in each area from the proportion who actually did go. The largest positive discrepancy was London North West at 17%. Other areas where more children went than might have been predicted included Surrey (+9%), London West (+8%), London North (+7%) and Leicester (+6%). Areas where fewer go than were predicted to go were headed by Yorkshire South (rounded to –9% on this map), Bristol (–7%), Essex South (–6%), Sheffield (–6%) and Nottinghamshire & Leicestershire North West (–6%). The map is shaded using two colours to highlight the divergence between places where many more and far fewer than the expected proportions went to university. Since the late 1990s geographical divisions in entry chances have reduced slightly, but remain similar. Social class thus still only explained part of the map of university entry for people aged around 30 in 2012.

What could have accounted for the remaining variation between these areas? The answer is likely to be many different things. There are often no simple single explanations to demographic patterns, and this is part of what makes the population of the UK so interesting. Analysing statistics such as these allows new ideas to be generated on the basis of current knowledge, which in turn can be analysed until there is little left to try to explain. For instance, the desire to leave the most remote parts of Scotland, North Wales, Northumberland and North Yorkshire could drive children to try particularly hard to get to university. The school segregation in other areas might influence their children to achieve lower than average marks in their exams (we look at GCSE exam results for this age group by these areas later). There are more university places in the South and centre of England and so more children from areas in this central belt might apply to universities as they are nearer home. There are many possible explanations.

The most important point that this introductory example makes is that it is not possible to reduce something as superficially simple as university entry into a purely social process whereby different social groups experience different chances and those social differences are what the map of university entry rates portrays. There is much more to the map of 18-year-olds' chances of attending university than that.

AN EXERCISE

(6 to 600 players)

You do not need a computer, or even a piece of paper and pen, to draw a map. Human bodies themselves will suffice. Here is a recipe for drawing a map of the geographical origins of a room of students. 'Cooking time' is about 10 minutes, although allow slightly longer when undertaking this exercise with over 100 students.

1   Each student needs to decide where they 'come from' (were born), i.e. their home city and suburb. If a student comes from outside the UK, that is fine – they will simply be appended to one of the edges of the map we are about to draw.

2 Determine the four corners of your map. Who comes from the furthest North East, North West, South East and South West? These four students need to move to stand at the top right, top left, bottom right and bottom left of the classroom/lecture theatre respectively.

3 Now all the other students must begin to sort themselves out in the map of where they come from. Begin by sorting yourselves out from North to South. The further North you come from, the further back in the room you need to be. Ask your neighbours directly in front of and behind you where they are from to work out if you are in the wrong place.

4 Now sort yourselves out from East to West. The further East you are from, the further right you should be along the row you are in. Again, by asking your neighbours (either side of you) where they are from, you should be able to work out if you are in the wrong place. Here left and right are as viewed by an observer looking at you from the front of the room.

5 Now check with all four of your nearest neighbours (those to your left and right and those in front of and behind you) to find out if they come from further East of you, further West, further South and further North of you respectively. If they don't, you need to move around a little more.

6 Finally, all shuffle in towards the centre of the room to end up with just an arm's length between you and your four nearest neighbours. Once you have done this you will have created a map of space in which the area in the room is arranged in proportion to the population of students in your class by their areas of origin.

Having created your own map of the UK, what you next use it for is up to you. If you are undertaking this exercise in an 'old university', your map is likely to include most of the UK as people tend to travel further away from their areas of origin. However, what are the geographical biases in your distribution? Where does the person in the centre of your map come from? Further South or North than most people in the country?

For reference, the central constituency in Figure 1.2 is the Peak District in Derbyshire (area 50). If you are undertaking this exercise in a school, then your map is likely to be of a only very small part of one country – but it is still a map drawn in proportion to you. Does the person in the centre of your map live closest to your school? If not, why not? Next you could begin to look for geographical differences among yourselves. If at university, then sit down if you took a 'gap year' before starting your studies. If at school, sit down if you intend to go to university (or take a gap year). Did more students to the South or North of your particular map of Britain sit down?

You could divide the class into groups depending on where they originate from and then poll those groups to see if there are differences in their attitudes, say, to voting. These polls can be done anonymously on scraps of paper. The point is that even within one room there are likely to be geographical patterns. These are patterns which cannot simply be explained by the social, economic or political backgrounds, statuses and beliefs of those being counted.

[Note: This game can easily be played for other countries and regions in the world if students have some link to those. If playing this game in the Southern Hemisphere, it is customary to place South towards the back of the room rather than North. An advanced version of the game, designed to simulate the panic that can ensue following epidemic disease outbreak, involves all students forming the original map as described above, but then trying to move to be as far away from their four geographical neighbours as possible while still remaining in the room. This version is best not played with students under age 18 or classes of more than 60 given the consequences.]

Conclusion

To understand the population of the UK you need to understand geographical and historical circumstances as much as social, political and economic processes. It can take a little time to get used to the social landscape of the UK if you have not seen it before. Look again at Figure 1.5 and follow this account of the human life-chance contours it reveals.

The social landscape is lowest, and the ground most fertile for prospective students, in a T-shaped valley which encompasses the northern and western suburbs of London stretching out from there to Oxford in the west and to Surrey in the south. Surrounding that valley is a plain only a little less fertile than the valley itself. From central London it reaches down to the Sussex coast, across the South Downs, up the Thames Valley to Hampshire, then across to Gloucestershire, Somerset, Dorset and Devon. The northern border of the plain stretches from Shropshire, through Herefordshire, Warwickshire, Northamptonshire, Leicestershire, Cambridgeshire, Bedfordshire, Suffolk, ending at the Essex coast. Around the plain are found the foothills of more stony ground where life chances are a little less sure for the children of North East and South East London, Kent, the Hampshire coast, Southampton, Wiltshire, Bristol, Cornwall and most of Wales, the Midlands and the North West of England.

The land of Britain tends to rise as you move northwards, both topographically and in terms of barriers to life chances. There is a particularly noticeable cliff in socioeconomic space as you cross into the north of Nottinghamshire and up to the highlands of Greater Manchester (East), into Sheffield, the rest of South Yorkshire and East Yorkshire. Further north the human geography of the land becomes mountainous again in Tyne & Wear and across most of Scotland, with the highest peak in the UK being Glasgow. Northern Ireland is part of the uplands. There are some dips within the North and West, but these are not extensive enough to form anything approximating the great southern plain and there is no fertile valley in the North. These dips include parts of Mid & West Wales, Cheshire, Central Lancashire, Northumbria, Southern Scotland and Edinburgh.

The human landscape of the UK is not dissimilar to its physical geography. However, even in the North, cities tend to have been built in small valleys whereas in this landscape they can form great mountains. There is no need for water to flow to the sea over a landscape made up of human chances. It is just fortunate from the point of view of engaging the imagination that, if you think of the River Thames running between South East and North West London, the human geography topology is also a plausible set of physical contours, although, had we the space to draw them, we would not draw rivers on the maps in this book but motorways, railways, airports and sea crossings. These are the rivers which carry people over the land. However, drawing these would have complicated the maps further.

Further Reading

Books like this one often tell you that there are many other books you should read. This is true, but usually unhelpful. Almost everyone who reads about further reading then ignores it. Many people are not like you and have already skipped this part. Congratulations, you are a little different, work harder and are more likely to be okay if you persevere. Of those who start off with similar life chances, born around the same time, in the same place and class, it tends to be the ones who persevere a little more who do better. However, those who try hardest but come from the poorer areas and classes tend to have worse chances than those who are a little lazier, but start off a bit more privileged. If you want an interesting place to go to begin reading about these issues and especially about how they influence people living in the UK, then I would suggest you start with the government statistical agencies' on-line publication *Social Trends*: http://data.gov.uk/dataset/social_trends. However, it can be a little dull, so if you want something more lively have a look at the work of the Equality Trust: www.equalitytrust.org.uk or, for the nearest thing to the nemesis of that Trust to be found amongst campaigning websites, visit: www.taxpayersalliance.com.

Key Point Summary

- It is helpful to look at the population of the UK with a map based on that population.

- Life chances can be shown on such a map, such as the chance of going to university.

- Such chances alter over time, across space and are often influenced by social class.

2

BIRTH

… and the suburban pied piper

This chapter begins the story of the population of the UK by starting with babies. The chapter ends by looking at where and when most of these children, as adults, have children themselves. Before that we consider demography's contribution to the patterns uncovered in Chapter 1, which are the products of many other patterns. If you are reading this book as a UK-born university student in the early years of the second decade of the twenty-first century in these countries, then by far the most important factor that resulted in you attending university was not how hard you worked, but what was the year of your birth. The more recently you were born, the more likely you were to attend university.

Figure 2.1 shows the numbers of babies born in each year of the last century in Britain. The cohort born in 1982, aged 30 in 2012, is highlighted. At the peak, 1.1 million babies were born in 1920, 300,000 more than in 1919. People waited until war was over to have children. Similarly, 150,000 more babies were born in 1946 as compared to 1945. Births peaked again in 1964 and 1990, with intervals of 18 years and then 26 years between these post-war highs as the average age at which women had children rose. This graph does not, of course, tell you what the fertility rates in different years were as there were growing numbers of women over the period. What it does tell you is that if you were a child born since the lowest birth year of 1977, then you belong to a cohort of children which was as small as those born over 50 years ago. There are about 200,000 a year (or more than one-fifth) fewer of you than there were in your parents' generation. That deficit reduced a little in the most recent decade as births rose to a new peak in 2008, but then fell again in 2009 with the recession (see further reading at the end of this chapter).

Why should the size of your birth cohort matter as compared to that of previous generations? Well, among many other things it will influence the chances and choices you later have over employment, the kind of home you can live in and your educational chances when the numbers of places at university are fixed (which may soon be changing). As a larger, older generation retires from work there are fewer young people to replace them. As the homes built for the larger families of the past are vacated there are larger houses to move into. But there are also fewer of you to care for a larger and ageing population, and fewer of you to have children yourselves.

When the first draft of this book was written, using data which was then available up to the year 2000, the government demographers were predicting the number of births that would continue to fall until around 2006, then rise slightly until 2020 before falling again to a new low in 2037. In the event almost the opposite occurred; there was an extraordinary economic boom, births rose very quickly from 2001 onwards, not falling slightly until 2009, around nine months after the economic crash of 2008), but then rose again in 2010. One cohort is singled out in Figure 2.1: those born in 1982, children who turned 18 in 2000, and in 2012 turned 30. We'll follow this year group below.

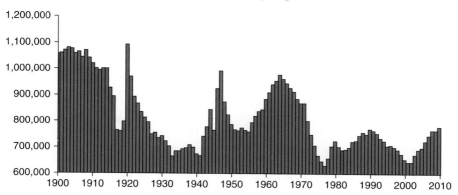

Figure 2.1   Number of live births in Britain, 1900–2010

Note: Cohort born in 1982, aged 18 in 2000 and 30 in 2012, is coloured red.

Source: ONS and GRO (Scotland) websites.

Having said that year of birth matters (given you were born in the UK), then for many things the next most important determinant of your life chances is whether you were born female or male. In every society sex influences differently how long you might live, what job you might have, and your educational chances. Intriguingly, the chances of which sex you are born have also varied over time. Slightly more babies have always been male but, as Figure 2.2 shows, the proportion of female babies has fallen over the course of the century from a high of 491 per thousand in 1900 to a low of 485 per thousand in the mid-1970s, rising slightly again to 487.7 per thousand by 2010. It is a very interesting question to ask why this should be so.

Because girls' survival rates are slightly better than boys', by age 21 the numbers of men and women living in the UK are almost identical. Compared to women born just seven years earlier, those women born in 1982, highlighted on Figure 2.2, will have a few less potential male friends, but a few more than women born seven years later will have.

If we turn to look at the key life chance this book began with – your chance of entering university – the importance of birth cohort size becomes apparent. The

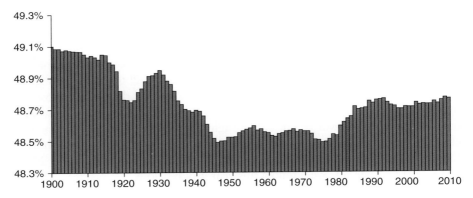

Figure 2.2 Proportion of live births that were female in Britain, 1900–2010

Note: Cohort born in 1982, aged 18 in 2000 and 30 in 2012, is coloured red.

Source: ONS and GRO (Scotland) websites.

first bar chart in Figure 2.3 shows the rise in the number of full-time undergraduate university places in the UK between 1970 and 2008 for men and women; the second shows the numbers of people turning 18, 19 or 20 in that year (estimated from the births occurring some 18, 19 and 20 years earlier); and the third chart shows the first figures as a proportion of the second set as a crude estimate of university entry rates. The simplicity of the estimate should be clear; the birth data does not include Northern Ireland, some children migrate or die before reaching 18 and increasingly undergraduates come from a greater age range than this (and more from abroad). However, the apparently smooth growth of the crude numbers of students is revealed to have instead been stagnation in the proportion of those born in the early 1950s and 1960s going to university. There followed a near doubling of the proportion of men and an even faster rise for women during the 1990s and further rises in the 2000s, with women being 15% more likely than men to become full-time undergraduates by 2008.

Our cohort, born in 1982, is highlighted again in this chart, but now just for women (the three pink bars outlined in red). See how in the first chart the number of places was almost 300,000 more for this group than for those born ten years earlier. Furthermore, fewer girls were born in the years 1980/81/82 than had been for any other cohort in the chart, only just over 1 million in those three years. These two things combined resulted in the equivalent of almost 60% going to university. In practice many of those 60% were not of that birth cohort and it would not be until 2010 that 50% of young women born in England were going to university in England, but the rise shown here, including overseas born students, is nevertheless remarkable.

Cohorts of students have been growing as the cohorts of the population as a whole are generally falling. The proportions becoming students have never been so high. These proportions are higher than those shown in Chapter 1 because overseas and Open University students are included here, as well as mature students, but part-time and further education students are omitted (these show even greater rises for women). At the start of the century only some 25,000 students attended university, under 1% of the equivalent population and almost all male. The proportion of those students who foresaw that women would out-number them by the end of the century is unknown. It was probably nearer 0% than 1%.

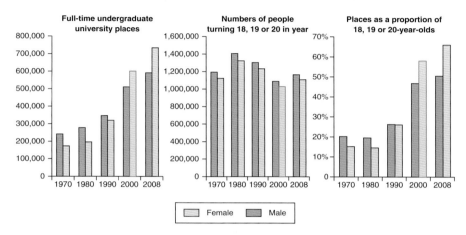

Figure 2.3 Students in the UK, cohort size and proportions, 1970–2008

Note: Figures are by entry year; women born in 1982 have their three bars outlined in red.

Source: Social Trends 32 and *41* and ONS and GRO (Scotland) websites.

It is perhaps in the years between birth and age 18 that a person's chances in life are largely set. The Jesuits famously said that if they were given a child until he was seven, they could give you the man. If you look back for evidence for this quotation, you may in fact find that they were actually saying they did not want to educate children before the age of seven, or girls at any age! Some believe that life chances are largely set before or by birth, while others argue that almost any children can learn without limits. In practice we do not tend to intervene in life systematically enough to fully test these arguments. Other than through adoption, we do not take children at young ages and place them in very different families to see what happens to them.

In Britain at any given time whether children achieve something such as going to university or not is largely determined by the family into which they are born. Families are far from idle in the education process. An increasing number pay for their children to attend private school to try to ensure things such as university entry. Others pay for home tutoring, provide additional teaching themselves or bribe their children to 'try harder'. Still more improve their children's chances by moving geographically so that their children go to a supposedly better school. Like cattle moving up to higher slopes for new grass in the summer, a large proportion of the children of Britain are herded into fresh pastures as they age. This migration of school-age children and their parents is one of the most significant population movements in Britain, and so this is where we turn to next.

The pattern in Figure 2.4 shows that it was in 1996/97 that children's chances of going to university were most influenced by their family backgrounds, for those people born in 1978. Each year after that child's parents' job had a little less influence on whether he or she would go than before, but the social divisions established by 1996/97 were very strong and had a long legacy. Parents began to move house more often to try to ensure that their children grew up near other children who had better life chances. Let's have a look a few years on from those bars shown above, at when children who became adults in 2000 were born in 1982. We begin with some 683,464 babies.

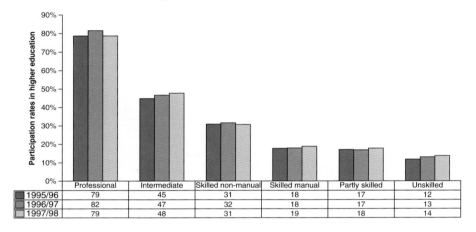

	Professional	Intermediate	Skilled non-manual	Skilled manual	Partly skilled	Unskilled
1995/96	79	45	31	18	17	12
1996/97	82	47	32	18	17	13
1997/98	79	48	31	19	18	14

Figure 2.4 Participation in higher education by social class, 1995–98

Note: Social class is assigned through information collected by the Youth Cohort Survey on the occupation (using Standard Occupational Classification categories) of parent or guardian with the highest income in the household.

Source: Department for Education and Skills; Office for National Statistics; Universities and Colleges Admission Service; *Social Trends 30;* HEFCE Consultation paper, Supply and demand in higher education, HEFCE 01/62, 2001.

In Figure 2.5 the count of babies born in 1982 is subtracted from the count of 18-year-olds living in Britain in 2000. The map suggests that there was indeed a significant movement out of the cities from birth. This was highest in London South Inner where 9001 babies were born, but only 5544 18-year-olds remained. This is shown on the map as a large net outflow. It is thus a flow of −3457. Birmingham East and Glasgow recorded the next largest net outflows. The three largest net inflows were in Dorset & Devon East, Devon & East Plymouth and Somerset & North Devon.

The flight to 'better schools' is only one of the factors underlying the movements shown in Figure 2.5, but it is probably the key factor. The Figure only shows net change. It hides a huge amount of gross change. In many places (as shown in Figure 2.7 below), for every child that moves out of an area, another child (and its family) moves in to take its place. There are relatively few new homes being built and relatively few (although growing) areas and neighbour-hoods being abandoned in Britain.

The way in which children are sorted by education is largely a zero sum game. More go to university each year and fewer leave schools with no qualifications, but the meanings of having a degree or of having no qualification also alter over time. There are only a fixed number of chairs in the classrooms of the 'better schools', although more of these seats have bums on them than in other schools. By definition, half of all children in Britain have to go to below-average schools. Where education remains a social sorting exercise and school league tables are still published, this cannot be stopped. It has stopped for some in Wales, where tables are not published, but migration during childhood was also lower in Wales before then.

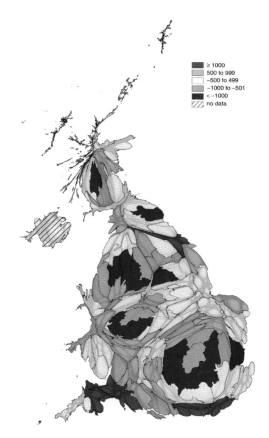

Figure 2.5 Where 18-year-olds moved to (and where they left), net numbers since birth

Note: Counts by European Constituency area.

Source: Estimated from school rolls of 15-year-olds in 1997 less the count of babies in the 1981 Census.

Figure 2.6 suggests school exam results are almost certainly influencing both the directions in which children migrate and how that migration influences the examination results. The degree of variation in the graphs implies that there is a little more going on here than a very simple geographical relationship (that is the subject of the next chapter). Every year several thousand children move out of areas where high numbers are not awarded good school grades at age 15 or 16. Hence the areas when plotted as points in the graph in Figure 2.6 tend to be scattered along a line.

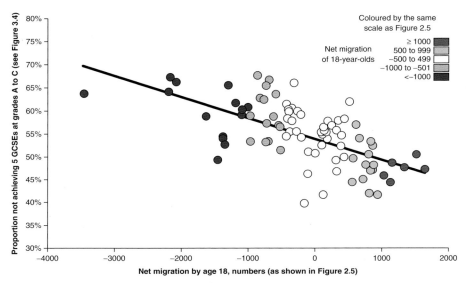

Figure 2.6   Net migration to age 18 (1982–2000) by GCSEs at age 15/16

Note: Each point is a 1999 European parliamentary constituency in Britain.

Source: 1981, 1991 and 2001 Censuses; analysis of national school league tables for Britain 1993–99.

The crude net migration statistics hide very much larger gross flows of children. Figure 2.7 shows the numbers of children moving into each part of Britain for every 100 moving out. Over an 18-year period large numbers of children do move towards areas where fewer are awarded high grades at school, just fewer than those who move out. Even the pattern shown in this figure is a net pattern. If this were the exchange of children between areas every year, many city centres would soon become childless! What prevents that is that these centres are repopulated by births (Figures 2.8 and 2.10 when combined show how very high numbers of births are added to Central London's population each year, explaining how its very low 78% child replacement rate through in-migration can be maintained over time).

It is babies, younger children, the children of immigrants and the children of families who find that they have become poorer who replace most of the more affluent children who are leaving the city centres every year. The overall geography

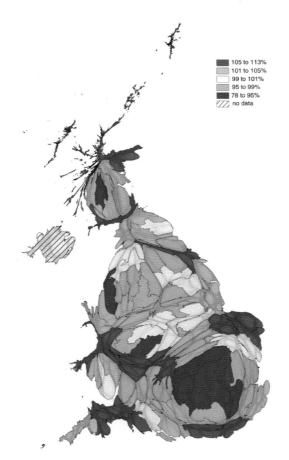

105 to 113%
101 to 105%
99 to 101%
95 to 99%
78 to 95%
no data

Figure 2.7   In-migration of children as proportion of out-migration

Source: 1991 Census special migration statistics children aged 1–15.

of where children live is altering slowly too, but the vast majority of annual migration is required just to keep the social system static – so that affluent areas stay affluent and poor areas remain poor.

The particular group of babies we are following (those born in 1982) didn't just grow older and move. Most have now had children, many only recently, but a few had children at a much younger age than others. There is a very strong geographical pattern to Figure 2.8, which shows the number of babies born to teenage mothers in each area between 1991 and 1998. The map is an approximation of the distribution of 18-year-olds in 2000 who are themselves already parents. A very clear north–south divide runs though the map, dividing areas where fewer than 4000 babies have been born to teenage mothers from areas where up to over 7000 babies have young mothers (we don't know the age of many of the fathers). The East of London is the main exception to this divide where rates of teenage pregnancy are comparable to the North of England, Scotland and Wales (we can talk of rates as these areas have roughly equal populations).

Compare Figure 2.8 to Figure 1.5 in the previous chapter of the proportion of 18-year-olds entering university in 2000. The two maps appear to be rough mirror images of each other. The places from which children are more likely to get to university are the places where they are least likely to have children young. Are there really such different geographically separated groups of children in Britain following markedly divergent paths through life?

■	≥ 7000
■	6000 to 6999
▦	5000 to 5999
▨	4000 to 4999
□	< 4000
▨	no data

Figure 2.8   Babies born to teenagers in Britain, 1991–98

Note: Counts by European Constituency area.

Source: Birth records by mother's age at birth.

Figure 2.9 provides a clearer way of assessing whether the two geographical distributions do tend to be the inverse of each other than can be achieved by visually comparing the two maps on which the figure is based. It suggests that there is a clear inverse relationship with all areas in Britain lying close to that

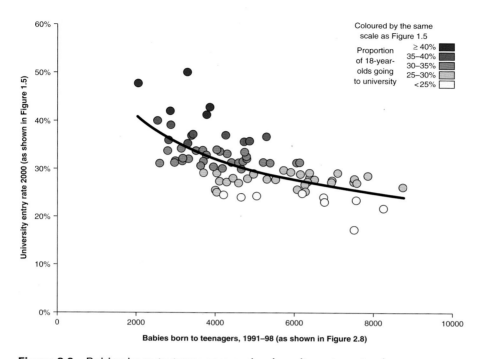

Figure 2.9 Babies born to teenagers and university entry rates by area

Source: ONS and GRO (Scotland) websites; successful UCAS under age 21 applicants from National Statistics website and estimated for Scotland and Northern Ireland; birth records by mother's age at birth.

trend. There are no places where a higher than average number of teenagers have children and a higher than average proportion go to university, and no areas where few teenagers have children and a low proportion go to university. This is a little surprising as these are large geographical areas and only a minority of children go to university (in all but one of the places) and only a very small minority of teenagers have children.

Most children by the age of 18 neither go to university nor have children of their own (although a very small number do both). The graph in Figure 2.9 suggests that similar processes underlie what makes it more or less likely for children to take different paths through life, and these processes are at play across the whole of the UK and are strong enough to result in quite a uniform distribution of life chances by area. Everywhere where there were more than 6000 births to teenagers had a university entry rate below 30% in 2000. Nowhere where the university entry rate was above 40% were more than 4000 children born to teenagers over these eight years in the 1990s.

One argument is that the British education system, and what underlies it, is largely responsible for these patterns. The next chapter elaborates on that. Here the supposition that it is current educational expectations and norms that are influencing so much else can be claimed to hold for many of the women who only have children later in life (or never at all). This is a group who are often portrayed as having the most choices in life, but they often look, in aggregate, to have the least.

Figure 2.10   Babies born to mothers aged 35 or over, 1991–98

Note: Counts by European Constituency area.

Source: Birth records by mother's age at birth.

Figure 2.10 shows how older mothers and their children are crowded into London and the Home Counties of England. Look at Figure 3.9 to compare these distributions to that of where university graduates end up living in Britain. For many people reading this book, this is the pattern of your mother's geographical choices. For an even larger proportion, this will be where you have children. The more likely you are to be reading this book, the more likely you are to have children later in life yourselves and the more likely are your children to be born in the areas shaded darker in Figure 2.10.

A significant number of people have no children of their own at any point during their lives, and that number is growing. It is growing partly out of choice, but also because more and more people find it difficult to have children when they stop using contraceptives to try to conceive at older ages. Others think or are told that they cannot afford to become parents. The area with the lowest proportion of children of all between ages 5 and 17 – and the highest proportion of women of child-bearing age (20–44) – is London Central.

AN EXERCISE

(20 to 100 players)

Form yourselves into the map of Britain or your local area according to your place of birth as described at the end of Chapter 1. Now, put up your hands if you moved home in your first year of life. Quite a few of you should have done this. Parents often find the home they are in unsuitable for a small baby, or need to move home urgently to get more space. Now raise your hands if you moved in your second year of life, third year, fourth year, fifth year and so on. Is there any pattern to when your parents moved home? Did those living closest to city centres or who were first-born children move earlier? What about the direction of travel? How many moved towards the centres of towns and how many into the suburbs? Next, everyone with their hands up needs to move around the room, each in a precise direction, so that the map is reformed by where you had moved to in your first few years.

By now you should all be located according to where you first went to school by age 5. Carry on the exercise, raising your hands if you moved, or moved again, at ages 6, 7, 8, 9, 10 or 11. There might be a sudden increase in the later two years. It depends partly on what kind of education system was in place where you lived at this time, but in many areas where you go to secondary school depends on where you lived at age 10. Obviously having older brothers and/or sisters complicates that picture, as do parents separating. A more sophisticated form of this exercise would have you playing the part of your oldest sibling. Age 10 is a peak year for migration in Britain. Reform the map to reflect your distribution by age 11.

Carry on to 12, 13, 14, 15, 16, 17. Do you notice any unusual changes in direction here? These are often the ages at which families are most settled geographically, but you might notice quite a few people moving home between age 15 (GCSE year) and the start of AS and A-level studies. Finally, if you are in an old university, note the high migration rates of almost all of you at age 18 or 19. For those who doubt the importance of education on migration (and migration on education) ask yourselves why Britain runs a system, unlike almost any other in the world, in which between one-third and half of its 18-year-olds are expected not only to leave home, but often to leave the village, town or city they grew up in and be scattered across the UK in a way which appears random, but which you will know (if you have applied to university) is incredibly closely controlled by A-level grades and quotas. The quotas might well be about to go, but exam grades might matter more than ever before as a result of other changes in student funding coming in from October 2012. If you are reading this book in Scotland or Ireland, your experience may be more like that found elsewhere in the world and you are unlikely to have moved as far from home. The same will be true if you are attending a 'new' (i.e. post-1992) university.

Finally, go forward in time and predict where you will be at ages 20, 21, 22, 23, 24, 30, 40, 50, 60 and 70. Will you be part of the majority who fit the stereotypes being described here or do you think you may be a little different? (Most people think they will be different. Most, of course, are not.)

Conclusion

The four maps in this chapter each show a different relationship between one aspect of life chances in Britain and the underlying landscape of opportunity to attend university. Figure 2.5 shows that there is a general tendency for children to flow downhill between birth and 18 towards areas where they are more likely to win university places. There are exceptions to that rule. It does not hold for the Oxford, Surrey and North West London 'social valley', which was described as the most fertile area of the landscape at the end of the last chapter. As the next chapter makes clear, doing well here often comes at a price that your parents have to pay (Figure 3.6) and many of the children whose parents cannot pay that price do particularly badly in this part of the UK (Figure 3.3). Thus many parents move themselves and their children out of the valley to 'better schools'. Similarly, there are a few areas, almost all in the South, into which more children are moving than leaving; this appears not to be in aggregate to their collective benefit (if entry to university is seen as important). However, read a little further on and you'll find that these are often good places to be at age 15 rather than 17. The variation shown in Figure 2.6 is largely explicable when such other geographies are also considered.

  Figure 2.8, showing where teenagers have the most babies, follows the contours of the landscape more closely but also reveals a north–south divide which is stronger than our underlying geography of opportunity. Most teenagers who are likely to become young parents do not go to university whether they have children or not, and so there are other factors at play in creating this pattern of chances. The importance that the landscape retains is revealed by Figure 2.9, but the other factors that account for the variation in that figure are again clearly geographically determined. If they were not, then the spatial pattern shown in the map would not be so clear.

Where children are most encouraged and cajoled to study hard, where their schools are most likely to be 'good', where their teachers have more time and are perhaps a little better equipped, where their parents are most able to help them and have the greatest incentives to do so, where children are most expected to go to university, is where most do. And what might underlie all these things? Most probably the answers involve the same forces that encourage women in these places to have children late in life. The next seven chapters explore just a few of the forces, facets and relationships revealed to be influencing the population.

Further Reading

The *Guardian* Datablog ('facts are sacred') birth statistics: 'The ONS has released data on birth rates for 2009, showing a slight drop year on year but a rise over the past decade', posted by Kate Stoddard on Tuesday, 25 May 2010. Here is where you'll find it: www.guardian.co.uk/news/datablog/2010/may/25/birth-rate-statistics-england-wales.

And if you are interested in why the ratio of boys to girls born varies over time, think about this: 'One index of social health is the number of boys born in comparison to girls. Because the male foetus is more vulnerable to maternal stress, women produce fewer boys when times are hard. (For example there is often a fall in the ratio of boys to girls a few months after disasters such as earthquakes and the terrorist attack on 9/11). In England and Wales the highest ratio of boys to girls occurred in 1973. In terms of contented mothers it was the best of times.' Read the full article and the evidence it presents here: www.familyandparenting.org/Parenting/Tavistock+Clinic (posted by Sebastian Kraemer during 2011).

Key Point Summary

- The number of babies born alters over time, as does the proportion born female/male.

- Children migrate in directions which are predictable in aggregate, out of city centres.

- Babies are most likely to be born to older mothers in the South East of England.

3

EDUCATION

... the sorting out of children

In most schools in Britain children are sorted into groups according to how able they are deemed to be. They are tested at various points through examinations, and those test results are used to sort them further and to determine whether they will be permitted to progress on to each next stage after the end of compulsory schooling at age 16. For those who leave school at age 16, 17, 18 or 19, the results of these tests are used to curtail their employment or further education options. Then, for the large numbers who go to university from age 18, they are subjected to further tests.

Almost all university tests are designed so that almost no one is allowed to fail, but students are still crudely graded at age 21 (around 90% are awarded what is called a 'second-class degree'). Thus, by age 21, almost every child in Britain has been labelled as inadequate in some way – from not being awarded any qualifications at all, to being labelled as second class. This might appear a little odd, especially if you are not familiar with the way things are done in Britain. The overall effect is to put almost everybody in their place socially, through a system labelled 'education'.

Throughout this book I have been assuming that you are aged between about 16 and 20 and are reading this in Britain in the second decade of the twenty-first century. Given that you are reading this book, you almost certainly took General Certificate of Secondary Education examinations (GCSEs) when you were aged around 15/16 (Standard Grade examinations in Scotland). If you are reading this book from outside Britain, it might be useful to know that these are also known as 'Key Stage 4 exams'.

A National Curriculum came into force in Britain in 1992 to ensure uniformity over what all state school pupils were taught and, by 1995, pupils aged 11 at primary schools were beginning to be examined nationally at what is called 'Key Stage 2'. In many ways KS 2 represented the reintroduction of the old 11-plus examination, which determined many older people's chances in life (and which still exists in a few parts of England). KS 2 differs in that it is not a 'last chance' as the old 11-plus became, but the first important exam of a series of exams for what have probably become one of the most examined sets of children in the world (KS 1 was just a 'warm-up').

The first of the 'most examined British generation' were the children who took KS1 in 1991, KS2 in 1995, KS3 in 1998, KS4 in 2000, AS levels in 2001, A levels in 2002, and – for the minority who had got this far – entered university in summer 2002. They were the first-year university students I was teaching while I wrote the first edition of this book. They looked a little washed out and were a little better behaved than their predecessors were, but they were no more clever or imaginative or insightful than them. What, then, was the purpose of so many examinations? To see this we need to look at where children are failed at each Key Stage of the process.

For most children in Britain the first examinations that really matter are those taken at age 11. These influence the 'sets' they will be placed in later in school, and if you are not placed in a high set it is very hard to do well later on. You might have thought that at this age we would be encouraging children; not so. For adults in their late twenties today, Figure 3.1 shows their numbers when, as 11-year-old children, some were deemed to have done well in these exams compared to others deemed to have done poorly. Only in one constituency (Surrey had a score of 1.08) were slightly more children awarded grades to indicate that they did well as opposed to poorly. The other extreme was found only a few miles away across the capital in London North East, where three children were deemed to have done poorly for every one who did well.

When a more detailed geographical level is examined, places ranking at the extremes were found to be closer still. Using parliamentary constituencies, ratios of achievement at age 11 were highest in England in Sheffield Hallam, where 2.2 children did well for every one who did badly, and lowest a few hundred metres away in Sheffield Brightside at 0.1 (one doing well for every ten who did badly)! The Sheffield average, of 0.45, means little for what (at age 11) had been the most educationally divided city in England (if private schooling is ignored). At a lower level still, half of all the children who did well in Sheffield city lived in just seven of the city's 29 wards in 1998. Since then there have been great increases in state spending in the poorer parts of Sheffield and the gap closed steadily between 1998 and 2010. Scotland and Wales are blank on the map in Figure 3.1 because, probably sensibly, their parliament and assembly did not favour releasing this information, but again spending on state education increased in both countries, and results improved as a result.

Around 200,000 children left school with no qualification from the areas shown in Figure 3.2 between 1993 and 1999. By 2012 they were aged between 28 and 35. Most still live nearby and still have no qualifications. Their distribution at age 16 could largely be predicted from the proportions deemed to have failed KS 2 some five years earlier. However, there are nine constituencies where such an exercise would under-predict the proportion (by between 3.7%

and 2%: Merseyside West, Leeds, Greater Manchester Central, Yorkshire West, Tyne & Wear, Yorkshire South, Sheffield, Cleveland & Richmond, East Yorkshire & North Lincolnshire) and three where the proportions would be over-predicted (by 2.3% to 2%: Cornwall & West Plymouth, Suffolk & South West Norfolk, Essex North & Suffolk South).

Figure 3.1   Children doing well at age 11 per child doing poorly, 1998

Note: Ratio of numbers achieving a score greater than four to those achieving less than four in 1998.

Source: Key Stage 2 results from neighbourhood statistics website.

It is mostly the impact of migration which helps to make Figure 3.2 a map with a simpler pattern as compared to that seen in Figure 3.1. But how is it possible that so many children were leaving school without a single qualification while the numbers receiving university degrees were accelerating (shown back in Figure 2.3)? The data used here does not include children attending those special schools where GCSEs were often not taken. Almost all these children were capable of passing some exams, but none passed.

Figure 3.2 Children achieving no qualifications by age 15/16, 1993–99

Note: The proportions of children receiving no GCSE results are shown.

Source: Analysis of national school league tables for Britain 1993–99.

In the 1990s, on top of the 200,000 a year given no awards at all, a further 200,000 children a year left school with only a few qualifications, less than five GCSEs at any level. That number has fallen in more recent years (see Further Reading section below) but the maps remain very similar. In Figure 3.3 the low-qualified are combined with those receiving no qualifications, totalling over one in seven of all children in 1990s Britain. Such low qualifications disbarred these children from most jobs that required developing further skills, such as basic secretarial work or working for a large firm in the building trades.

Figure 3.3 is not a map of ability. Children in Glasgow are not many times less able than those growing up in the Highlands of Scotland, as the map might be thought to imply. It is instead a map of migration and money. In the Highlands of Scotland, due to the sparsely populated nature of that land, parents have little choice over where to send their children to school and so there are no schools deemed to be 'failing'. In a compact city such as Glasgow, short geographical distances (and often having more money) allow parents to send their children to particular schools, allowing other schools to 'fail' disastrously. Parents can migrate out of the city while still commuting to work within it and so many take their children away from areas thought to be detrimental to their education. Underlying all of this, however, is the nature of these examinations. These examinations were designed to fail a certain proportion of children and to give low grades to yet more.

Figure 3.3   Children achieving few qualifications by age 15/16, 1993–99

Note: The proportions of children receiving less than five GCSEs at level A–G are shown.

Source: Analysis of national school league tables for Britain 1993–99.

Examinations where almost no one fails are possible and are the norm where students pay for their education in both fee-charging universities and private schools. People will not pay to be given a label saying they have failed. However, if examinations did not label a proportion of children as failing, then it would

Figure 3.4 Children achieving low qualifications by age 15/16, 1993–99

Note: The proportions of all children receiving fewer than five A–C GCSE results are shown.

Source: Analysis of national school league tables for Britain 1993–99.

not be possible for other children's parents to claim that they had 'done well'. Why we fail quite so many is more difficult to understand.

Figure 3.4 adds to Figure 3.3 all those who did not achieve what was seen as the basic school-leaving qualification of at least five GCSEs at levels A–C. This is loosely equivalent to the old school-leaving examination that existed before O levels were introduced. More than 55% of all children failed to reach this level in the period shown here (to include Scotland, which uses a different examination system, it is assumed that a standard grade 2 is equivalent to C and a 4 to G). The proportion in Britain failing at this level fell from 59% to 51% over the period mapped here, and continued to fall to reach 44% by 2011. The apparent achievement can be partly illusory because, at the other end of the education ladder, more go on to take university degrees of many kinds. As the bottom rungs of the ladder are lowered, the top is stretched further and further into the distance. In the near future achieving only five GCSE A–C grades will be seen as failure. By 2011, 50% of all children had, as 19-year-old adults, gained A levels or the equivalent of A levels.

For some children in Britain achieving only five GCSE grades A–C has already been viewed as failure. Most obviously these included the 7% of children who attended private schools between 1993 and 1999 (a slightly higher proportion attend now). Figure 3.5 shows that 83% of former private school pupils, aged 28–35 in 2012, achieved at least five A–C's, more than twice the proportion attending comprehensive schools and three times the number sent to secondary moderns (schools which are a relic of the old 11-plus system).

Although much is written on parents who opt out of the state system to send their children to private schools and the supposedly unfair advantage they then gain, their numbers are dwarfed by the quarter of all children who took their GCSEs in a state-funded school that practised some kind of discrimination on entry. Many of these are the so-called church schools. In general these schools exclude what they see as less able children, and consequently a majority of their pupils in the 1990s did well at GCSE by the standards of

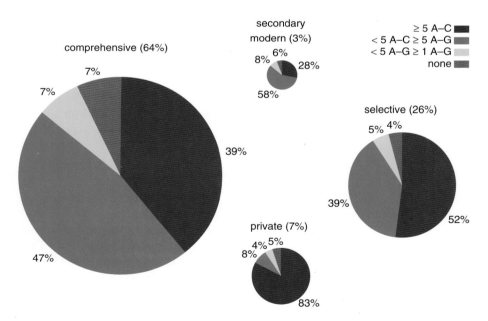

Figure 3.5   Children aged 15/16 by school type and GCSEs, 1993–99

Note: Charts are drawn in proportion to total numbers of children attending each type of school and shaded by the shares awarded particular grades.

Source: Analysis of national school league tables for Britain 1993–2000.

those days. They also had the lowest proportion receiving no qualifications of all the four types of school.

Today many more children attend discriminatory (or selective) state-funded schools (including many Academies), and a few more attend private schools than did in the 1990s. For those who doubt the effect of selection, whether it is state-funded or private, the figures for secondary modern schools in Figure 3.5 show what occurs when a school is truly labelled as being a 'failure'. Almost three-quarters subsequently 'fail'. British education has been set up in such a way that a minority of children can only succeed if others are deemed to have failed. Success can be aided by migrating, and millions of children are moved to new homes every year to aid this process.

Allowing schools to discriminate with their entry can aid success and success can also be bought by parents through the private system. However, purchasing opting-out of the universal system aids the failure of many who remain in it. Cities such as Oxford and Bristol have sent remarkably few children to university from all those born and brought up there. It is hard to find a cause other than the very high rates of private school opt-out in those cities. Similarly, it is hard to ascertain why more children from Sheffield go to university in comparison, despite it being a poorer and also greatly educationally divided city (other than Sheffield as a whole benefitting from there being so few private schools within its boundaries).

Although a fraction under 7% of children attended private schools at age 15 in the 1990s, that proportion disguises highs of 22% in London Central and lows of near 0% in several other places (Figure 3.6). Given that it is in central London that incomes have risen most since then, it is very likely to be in central London where there has been more of the slight increase in private school attendance. However, at the time of writing the 2011 census data had yet to be released confirming how many children of school age live in each area.

Parents fear for their children's life chances more in urban areas and so opt to try to pay to improve them most in those areas, further damaging already disadvantaged local state schools by withdrawing their children. However, private education is limited to those able to afford to pay. The proportion of children attending private schools in Edinburgh is higher than in Glasgow, as there are more wealthy people in the Scottish capital. Across Britain, private schools dominate in the South of England, even in areas where results overall appear fine. Money can buy your children out of the secondary school education lottery, but what exactly is it buying them into? Do children from private schools who attend university feel that they have succeeded or simply that they have just achieved what was expected of them?

Before turning to further and higher education it is worth briefly considering how the 1990s trends at age 15/16 have contributed to the current map of so-called educational achievement. Figure 3.7 shows the annual fall in the proportion of children failing to achieve the basic standard of five A–C grades between 1993 and 1999. Each year a slightly higher proportion of children was allowed to pass exams than the year before. Whether this reflected improving ability, better teaching or lowering standards could be argued to have been largely unimportant to children's life-chances as the worth of these exams fell in almost direct proportion to the additional numbers allowed to pass them.

Figure 3.6 Children attending private schools at age 15, 1993–99

Source: Analysis of national school league tables for Britain 1993–99.

The 'improvement' shown in Figure 3.7 was not evenly spread across the UK when expressed as a decline in the proportion who 'fails'. It was highest in the South of England and Wales. It was lowest in the North and in most of Scotland. It was low, too, in odd places such as Hampshire North & Oxford (but note the comment on Oxford schools above). This figure has to be read in conjunction with Figure 3.4 to see both where children's life-chances, as influenced by GCSEs, were best and worst, and whether they were improving or worsening in relative terms. The changes shown in Figure 3.7 have influenced the lives of millions of adults in Britain. Those aged around 30 in 2014 will appear better qualified as opposed to their older brothers and sisters, but worse qualified than younger adults are. This all occurred as the trends shown in Figure 3.7 continued through the 2000s when GCSE results improved rapidly in line with increased spending on hiring more teachers and teaching assistants in state primary and secondary schools.

≥ 3%
2.5 to 3%
2 to 2.5%
1.5 to 2%
< 1.5%
no data

Figure 3.7 Annual decline in children given low qualifications 1993–99

Note: Average fall in the numbers receiving lower than five A–C GCSE grades at age 15/16 as a proportion of those numbers.

Source: Analysis of national school league tables for Britain 1993–99.

For those who are deemed to do well at 15, what and where next? The numbers of these students who then went into sixth-form colleges, further education institutions and, three or four years later, to higher education institutions are shown in Figure 3.8 – some three million people in 2001. The geographical

Figure 3.8 Students aged 16+ in education in 2001 (numbers)

Source: Analysis of the 2001 Census Key Statistics by local authority.

clustering is due to the locations of large universities. Half a million people aged 16 or over became students in London. There are both more universities and a higher proportion of children staying on at school in the South and so the numbers are generally higher there. But have they succeeded?

Of those who stayed on at school but who did not go to university, most were to be awarded relatively low grades, implying failure as compared to their peers. Some may be qualified to work behind the counter in a bank or join the police force. Very few children who gain high A-level scores leave school on a winning streak and find a job. Instead, most now go to university. Once there they at least know they are almost certain to be awarded a degree if they do not drop out, and this, for these young adults in the recent past, qualified them for jobs their counterparts could not dream of applying for (fast-track promotion in a bank or the police force, for instance).

In the recent past many university students initially landed what for them were menial jobs such as working in a call centre. Almost all will have been awarded that second-class degree, worth far less than that of their parents, if they too went to university. Since 2008 the situation has been changing rapidly and jobs have been much harder to come by, even for the most qualified young adults. Suddenly a degree does not practically guarantee a job. Let's look back a few years to when it did.

Where did the minority of children who were awarded a degree in the early 2000s end up? A lot became doctors, specialist nurses, teachers, managers, engineers and the like, occupations often deemed more useful than cleaners, train drivers, builders and shop assistants, although how society would operate without the latter is hard to imagine. However, Figure 3.9 shows that the largest

≥ 150,000
125,000 to 150,000
100,000 to 125,000
75,000 to 100,000
< 75,000

Figure 3.9 University graduates aged 21+ in 2001

Notes: Counts by European Constituency area.

Source: Analysis of the 2001 Census Key Statistics by local authority.

geographical concentration of university graduates, almost one-third of a million, was found in central London.

Most graduates in London are engaged in making money out of other people: merchant bankers, accountants, international financiers, estate agents, staff of private firms' head offices and so on. By 2001, half of all graduates in Britain lived in just 30 European constituencies, only three of which were not in southern England (Northern Ireland is coloured dark in Figure 3.9 only because it is three constituencies worth of graduates combined). The meticulous sorting out of children resulted in eventually selecting this minority, many originally from the South of England, and enticing them to move to (or back to) particular parts of the South. The highest numbers of all were recently found in and around London; other areas have three to six times fewer.

Places cannot run without graduates, who include doctors and people who run power-plants, but they can get by with 50,000, as Figure 3.9 shows (roughly one-tenth of their populations). Ironically, perhaps, the greatest concentration of university graduates in 2001 lived in the same small area of the UK where 8% of children received no qualifications, 53% did not attain five GCSEs A–C and 22% of children were sent to private schools by their parents. A majority of parents having a university degree does not necessarily increase the chances of gaining a privileged education for large numbers of the children of others living there, it depends how mixed local schools are.

The last question for this series of figures, is how much has the map of graduates been changing? Figure 3.10 shows this. There were more than three times fewer graduates in 1971 as compared to 2001, but their geographical distribution was not dissimilar. In 1971, 3.5% of all graduates lived in London Central; by 2001 that had risen to 4%. Figure 3.10 shows this concentrating of graduates into London, to the detriment of the North, Scotland, Wales and the coastal fringes (including, already saturated, West Sussex and nearby East Surrey).

Thirty years of raising education 'standards', encouraging huge numbers of children to stay on at school (including raising the minimum age at which you can leave from 14/15 to 15/16 and, soon, higher), opening the university doors wider and giving out very many more degrees has resulted in a slight concentration of the pattern seen before all this began.

Our education system has been changed since 1971 in such a way as to maintain a process that sorts children into groups and then encourages those groups to move to particular places, mostly the same places as before, though now a few more arriving where there were most to start with. If so many more people are apparently learning so much more than people did in the past and passing so many more exams, why have the geographies changed so little over time?

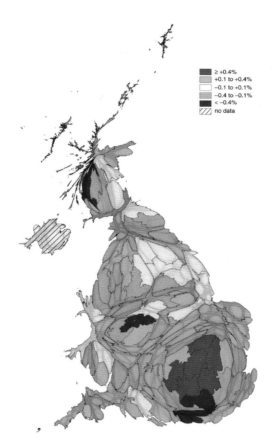

Figure 3.10   Change in area share of graduates aged 21+, 1971–2001

Note: Figures show the 2001 share of the total graduate proportion less the 1971 share.

Source: Analysis of the 2001 Census Key Statistics by local authority and the 1971 Census.

AN EXERCISE

(20 to 100 players)

Form yourselves into groups, each group containing just a few (three to six)
students. You could use the map you made at the ends of Chapters 1 and 2 to
form the groups so that they are made up of students who come from near one
another. Each group needs to imagine that all their members are aged 30, have
children of their own about to enter the education system and have somehow
come to political power. You are the slightly more grown-up children we have just
been describing; the ones who were in school in the 1990s, who were young
adults in the 2000s, who are mostly parents now.

As a group, you have ten minutes to complete the following task: 'Design an education system where the aim is to teach children rather than sort them. What role would exams take in such a system, if any? At what ages would you examine each child's ability, on what subjects/issues, and what proportions would you decide to fail at any stage? How would you decide who goes to university and which university they go to? How would you then grade university students?'

After ten minutes, stop and present your arguments to a neighbouring group. They, in turn, should present their suggestions to your group. Vote on the result and carry your combined most popular opinions forward to repeat the process after a further five-minute discussion (as a combined larger group of students). Then combine groups again and again until one set of ideas has won out. What led the most popular system to win through? Was it a good system, or simply well presented? Did you design it assuming your children were 'able'? Most parents think their children are above average!

Finally, take your initial groups and, at random, assign each group a (so-called) ability level. This is the level your prospective children could be expected to achieve under the current education system. One-third of all groups are now made up of the prospective parents of children who would attend university under the present system, one-third will not gain the qualifications to attend university but will be awarded five GCSE A–C grades, and the final third are the prospective parents of children who will not achieve this under the current system. Now, with your imaginary children in mind (and their interests at heart), each group needs to decide which of the systems initially presented it, in final consideration, thinks is best. Each group gets an equal vote. Vote on each system. Which system wins?

Conclusion

Surely some children 'succeed', you must be thinking, as not all are failed by education in Britain. Well, the above account is perhaps a little unfair on all the efforts of millions of school children, teachers, examiners, the writers of textbooks, and designers of education websites and television programmes to achieve an education. My view is that, often, despite the way in which most schools are organised and examinations imposed, many children still manage to learn, many teachers still manage to teach and far more people are better informed about the world than they were a generation ago. However, the basic purpose of the education system is still to put children in their place.

The key selection point has moved from age 11 in the 1960s to age 17 now. University admissions officers and those who control them are the gatekeepers to middle-class entry. A generation ago boys from Britain's top public schools did not need to go to university to maintain their status. Now even they have to go, and it would be almost unthinkable that a member of the royal family did not attend university. However, it would also be unthinkable if they were only allowed entry to the 'wrong' kind of university, and so we still run an ancient military academy to take those who need to avoid such a fate! Even that academy requires some entry qualifications and hence a few years ago one of its royal entrants was found to have been given a little more 'help' from his teachers with his A-level course-work than most students received. None of this is any child's fault. It is the fault of the adults who perpetuate such sorting of children, who ensure the existence of academies of lessons in killing, and who are currently exacerbating already obscenely elitist university hierarchies by introducing different fees for different universities.

Entry to university by A levels is simply entry largely according to school, which reflects parents' wealth through their ability to pay for their children's supposed exam success (by directly paying their school, through extra private tuition, or by paying more for their house in a better catchment area). Whenever someone suggests altering university entry systems away from A-level points there is uproar because the stakes are so high (the privileges of the children of the privileged).

Even as access was widened and more children from poorer backgrounds were allowed to attend university, a new divide began to form at age 21. Increasing numbers of students take a Master's degree after their first degree. Almost all of these have to be paid for privately. One, at least beneficial, effect of having an almost entirely private tier of education at age 21 is that it is at this level when the point is reached for the first time, that a majority are not labelled as having failed in some way. However, that will likely come next when they find it hard to secure jobs and almost impossible to secure the kind of job they may have once aspired to, at least when first looking.

Once you pay for your piece of paper, almost all of you are either passed or receive a distinction. There are no more second-class degrees when such large amounts of money are involved. Now that British universities are being privatised with fees of up to £9000 a year being introduced from 2012 onwards, we should expect the numbers of such degrees to diminish (at least in the more expensive universities). Can you imagine young adults accepting low marks for such high costs? And how much does it cost universities to award them higher marks? How much trouble might it cause not to?

The key age of selection and median school-leaving age increases by about a month every year. It currently stands at around age 17. Half-way through this century it should reach age 21 if the past century is any guide. The selective university sector was ever so slowly transforming itself away from the training ground of the elite and into what will become compulsory tertiary education – if current trends continued. Part of the reason for the introduction of differential fees in 2012 might have been a desire to try to halt this process, to halt the rise in the numbers going to university, but when jobs are scarce how many other palatable options do most young adults have?

Tomorrow's children face yet more years of examinations and an even more drawn-out process of being sorted out through education. That sorting out may well only be finished in the near future in their early twenties through postgraduate qualifications. And then, as now, it will not be by their efforts that they are sorted but mostly by their access to the resources needed to achieve such qualifications – their parents paying for those postgraduate degrees.

Further Reading

To update some of the statistics shown in this chapter, see Guy Palmer's poverty website. Apart from lots of useful facts about poverty it also tells you how Guy's career progressed (he went to Cambridge University) and why he now lives in Australia and has programmed his TV remote control to tell him when to plant vegetables in his garden. For that as well as the more serious statistics, see www. poverty.org.uk/30/index.shtml, where is said (in December 2011: 15):

> The proportion of 19-year-olds without Level 2 qualifications (effectively the same as '5 or more GCSEs or vocational equivalent'), has fallen sharply in recent years, down from one-third in 2004 to one-fifth in 2009. This fall at age 19 is consistent with the trend at age 16 (see the indicator on educational attainment at age 16).

> Although a half of young adults have not obtained Level 2 qualifications at age 16, this proportion reduces to one-fifth by age 21 (this data is for a cohort who were age 19 in 2007).

> Fewer 19-year-old girls lack Level 2 qualifications than boys: around 17% for girls at age 19 compared to 25% for boys.

> The proportion of 19-year-olds lacking Level 2 qualifications is somewhat lower in the South East than elsewhere in England.

> The lower a person's qualifications, the more likely they are to be unemployed and the more likely they are to be in low-paid work.

For details of the main political campaign aimed at ending the segregation of children between schools, see www.comprehensivefuture.org.uk, and for the opposing side see www.isaschools.org.uk.

Key Point Summary

- Most children in Britain either fail at school or are labelled 'second class' at university.

- The type of school a child in Britain attends has a huge influence on his or her exam results.

- Getting high exam results is more about social sorting than about being clever.

4

IDENTITY

... labelling people and places

People are given many kinds of label, and label themselves (and others) in many ways for many purposes. Some labels are harder than others to shake off or disguise – your sex and age, for instance. Others it is easier to keep confidential and hide if you wish, such as your religious beliefs and sexuality, although people may well make assumptions about you. Areas too can be labelled, based partly on the labels assigned to the people who live, have lived or will live within them. 'Gentrifying', 'growth' or 'up-and-coming' are labels given to areas through an assumption as to who their future inhabitants will be. Labels are central to studying the human geography of Britain; central in both trying to understand how labels come to stick and what useful meanings they might have.

There is often a great deal of truth behind what is sometimes called 'stereotyping' areas. There is also, of course, a great deal about the population of an area and the people with whom they interact that cannot be captured by a label, just as labelling individuals simplifies and masks their lives to a huge extent. However, a large part of the business of running society involves labelling. Chapter 3 could have been entitled 'the labelling of children'. Most labelling may well be unfair and unfortunate, but it is through labelling that society is run, that tasks are allocated (usually unfairly) and that the rewards of our efforts are distributed (almost always unfairly).

Labels matter. They may all be ephemeral, but that makes it even more crucial to understand them. Two centuries ago most social statistics did not include sex; it was irrelevant because women were seen not to matter. In two centuries' time they might not include sex again because sex will not matter. We can begin to trace, through the labels that are currently deemed to be of most importance, those categorisations which are used to control, blame and encourage people, and, above all, which are used to attempt to ensure that they conform.

In this chapter, ten key labels, which are taken from the 26 Key Statistics tables first released by the government from the 2001 census, are examined. These statistics are now a decade old. When the 2011 census is released all these maps can be updated. They will have changed a little. As I write, the 2021 census has been cancelled. It is claimed that the cancellation is to save money, but that cancellation was announced in 2011, long before any money would be saved. In 2022 students could be looking at maps like these, over a decade old, but would know that they cannot be updated.

Census statistics are vital to understanding the population of the UK, even the most basic numbers. Without a population census you cannot tell if life expectancy is rising or falling in different parts of the UK. Almost all of the other 16 Key Statistics 2001 tables not used in this chapter are used elsewhere in this book (Figures 3.8–3.10 have already used this same source). Government statistical agencies do not choose themes at random to publish. Government chooses to cancel censuses as much because its members do not want what they could reveal to be revealed, as to save money. The things which are counted are the things government (and the quasi-official bodies it consults) are convinced are key things which should be counted and published. Other statistics government needs but does not wish to reveal include most statistics on income and wealth.

In this chapter maps are shown of the labels that the powers that be wish us and our neighbours to know about. The ten labels range from what you might just think of as simple facts about yourself, to categories that you might object to having been put in. They are based on your occupation (or lack of one), the colour of your skin, your thoughts about a god, where you have come from and how alien that place (and you) appear to be, your living arrangements, who you share your bed and home with (or used to share with), and how posh or common you are deemed to be.

None of this information was collected clandestinely. It was all derived from your census form. Admittedly, the person in your household who completed that form could have faced a £1000 fine if they had not declared that information. Few people, however, may realise just how effective one little form duplicated almost 30 million times can be. The main alternatives to a census are either anarchy and an absence of planning, or a population register requiring some form of identification cards, either virtual or real. It is unclear in 2012 in which direction we are heading. A future government might well choose to reinstate the census.

Figure 4.1 uses the simplest census question to begin this illustration of place labelling. On the census everyone in Britain is labelled as either female (29,345,507 people) or male (27,758,420 people). The proportions are not equal because more men are born (Figure 2.2), but more men die young than do women and differing numbers leave and enter the UK at different times (only a tiny number change sex).

Nationally, by 2001, there were 94.6 men for every 100 women. The figure shows area deviations from that national proportion. The 42 areas with more than 94.6 men per 100 women are coloured light blue and the 43 areas with more women are coloured pink. This is a very crude form of area labelling. In theory, the presence or absence of a single man or woman in any area could swap its colour label over. However, in practice the method is quite robust. This is an unambiguous categorisation that gives a sex to all places. Only 15 places, categorised in this way, changed their sex over the 1990s decade and there is a pattern to the sex changes. Five mainly rural places became labelled 'male' as women left the place, and these women turned ten largely urban places 'female'. The most female place (52.9% female) in Britain today is Glasgow, the most male place is Thames Valley (50.1% female). At this scale, the gap of 2.8% is tiny, but with sex small things matter greatly.

Figure 4.1 Woman and men and the sexing of places in the UK, 2001

Note: Most unusually large group is shown when each place is compared with the UK.

Source: Analysis of the 2001 Census Key Statistics by local authority.

Just as places can be labelled according to the sex of their inhabitants, so too can they be labelled by their inhabitants' ages. Figure 4.2 uses the age categories included in the Key Statistics (except for amalgamating ages over 75 to allow comparison to be made with the past census figures). A place is given a specific age label if that age group is more in excess of its national proportion in that place than is any other age group there. Thus London East is coloured to show

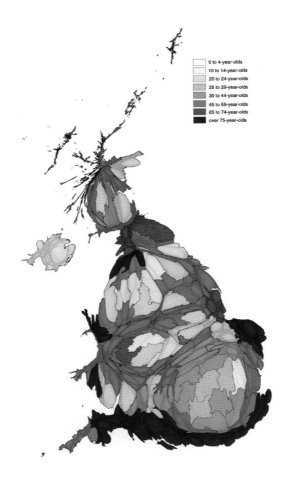

Figure 4.2 Age and the ageing of place in the UK, 2001

Note: Most unusually large group is shown when each place is compared with the UK.

Source: Analysis of the 2001 Census Key Statistics by local authority.

it is labelled '0–4' because that age group made up 6.5% of the population of that area in 2001, compared to 5.9% of the national population. The gap of 0.6% is greater than for any other age group in London East.

To be the atypical group that is used as an area label, it helps if the group is both large in number and unevenly spread across the UK. It is difficult for one particular group to be both things and so a diverse set of labels appear in these figures. In 1991 London East was labelled '65–74', as was Yorkshire West in 1971 (another of the three areas typified in 2001 as home to many babies), and Birmingham West was much older 20 years ago too. The labels of these areas have changed over time. Most areas, if labelled today following a new census, would be categorised by the same age group as ten years ago (so the place remains young or old as the people enter and leave it). Of those that have changed, most have aged slightly as the population as a whole ages and the local population has not been replaced by younger in-migrants.

Ethnicity is a label that was first used in the census in 1991; it is in use in Britain as a euphemism for race, which, for the census authorities in Britain, is seen as skin colour. Why the question came to be asked first in 1991 is a long and interesting story, but here we are most interested in the effects of that labelling.

Figure 4.3 uses the 2001 categories included in the Key Statistics amalgamated to their 1991 equivalents to allow the changing ethnicity of place to be assessed through the effects of these labels (the 2001 census included 'mixed' categories as the labels were changed to incorporate lighter coloured skins,

Figure 4.3 Ethnicity and the colour of place in the UK, 2001

Note: Most unusually large group is shown when each place is compared with the UK.

Source: Analysis of the 2001 Census Key Statistics by local authority.

including the Irish). Four of the ten comparable ethnic groups included are too evenly spread across Britain to label even a single place. One group, 'White', is so unevenly distributed that some 58 of the 85 areas have the highest excess as White. In 1991 it was exactly the same 58 places that were 'White'. The only changes to place labels have occurred within the minority of places labelled after 'minorities'. London Central, London South Inner and London North East were Black Caribbean in 1991; London North and London South East were Indian. These five areas' new colours can be read off the Figure. That three times as many places changed their sex over the same period is telling. Ethnicity is a label that sticks geographically.

Just as the census authorities introduced ethnicity as a new form of official identity in British social statistics in 1991, they – or, more strictly speaking, a few influential non-elected members of parliament (Bishops) – introduced

Figure 4.4 Religion and the spirituality of place in the UK, 2001

Note: Most unusually large group is shown when each place is compared with the UK.

Source: Analysis of the 2001 Census Key Statistics by local authority.

religion into the 2001 census. Strictly speaking (again), it had been asked before, but only in a special census held in 1851. Again the story behind this label is intriguing, but the motives of those involved are best revealed through the results.

Three of the nine possible religious labels describe people in groups either too small and/or too evenly spread across the UK to identify as places (Buddhists, people of 'other religions', and people who left the question blank – which was by law permitted only for this question). Of the six religions left, 'Christian' was the most unevenly spread, with a narrow majority of 44 areas, while the next largest group, of 22 areas, contained unusual numbers of people who explicitly said they were of no religion, or were Jedi (who were shamefully amalgamated with the atheists by the Whitehall unbelievers – people rarely rise high in the civil service if the force is with them ☺).

Geographically, 'no religion' matches the old (Wales and Scotland) and new (university city) non-conformist areas. Of the remaining areas in Figure 4.4, nine are Muslim, five Sikh, three Hindu and two Jewish. Within these 19 areas the beliefs of only 8% of their populations are used here to label some 13.4 million people's areas. Is this reasonable?

Sex, age, ethnicity, religion; what comes next? Are you married and just looking for fun or single and more serious about trying to start a relationship? If you are wondering what I am talking about, have a look at how people describe themselves in lonely-hearts columns. Identity is not just an official construct, we construct and publicise our own and others' identities daily. Identities also intermingle. Ethnicity, religion, age and sex are not independent. An old person is more likely to be female, white and Christian in Britain than is the population as a whole. She is also very much more likely to be widowed than is everyone else.

Figure 4.5 shows the unusual in the population geography of our quasi-legal/religious state of sexual availability and nest-building (and nest-breaking) by area. People, it would appear, are much more ready to remarry in the South of England as they age and as they move out of both cities and their initial relationships. The unusually high numbers of divorced people in three northern areas is not a reflection of the divorce rate but rather the reluctance of divorcees there to remarry. In the North and in the valleys of North Wales and Northumbria are found unusual numbers of widows (and a few widowers). There were, of course, once working slate and coal mines here, and other industries that contributed to very high premature male mortality in the past, but again it had to be coupled with a slightly higher northern and western reluctance to remarry.

There is an industry called geo-demographics, which classifies the population according to its postcodes. Figure 4.6 uses much larger areas than these and shows the 11 groups from within a classification of households that have a presence distinct enough for a place to be labelled after them. They have been ordered in crude life-stage order on the key to Figure 4.6. Here in this text let us add some labelling letters: from lone parent [A], to 'Other with kids' [B], all the

Married
Remarried
Divorced
Widowed
Single

Figure 4.5 Single, married, divorced, remarried and widowed in the UK, 2001

Note: Most unusually large group is shown when each place is compared with the UK.

Source: Analysis of the 2001 Census Key Statistics by local authority.

way through to lone pensioner [G], these groups form a rough demographic order, although few people ever move through all these life-stages.

To illustrate how geo-demographics works, pretend you are the extremely atypical person who behaves exactly socially and geographically as the geo-demographers might wish. You could, for instance, be born to a lone parent [A] in Greater Manchester (East) who then moves in with her mum [B] living in Yorkshire West before she finds a man, marries [C] and settles down back in Lancashire South. Not wanting to go too far from home you become a student [D] in Sheffield, get a job and live in a mixed household [E] in London North before saving enough for the deposit on your own flat [F] slightly further out, in London North West. You meet your soul-mate, sell the flat and move into his or her place [G] in Bristol. I'll let you complete the story, safe to say you'll end up alone on the coast.

Again, of course, it may be a very small but unusual extra number of households living in a place that lead it to be labelled in this way in these kinds of
maps. Wales is not a land of lone pensioners and lone parents as a cursory
reading of Figure 4.6 might suggest! These are just the two groups most over-
represented in the five Welsh European constituencies. Geo-demographics
emphasises what is unusual about the population of each place. In truth, there
are more similarities than differences between all places.

Did you notice all that moving about your hypothetical geo-typical alter-
reality engaged in? That was not extreme. For places to have social definition
people need to keep moving. Chapter 2 explored this in detail for children.

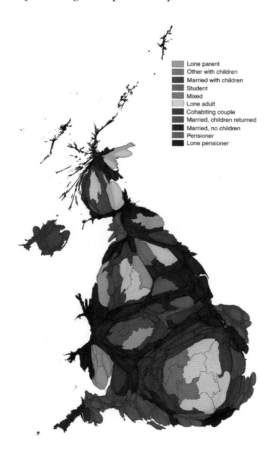

Figure 4.6 Through the keyhole: household composition in the UK, 2001

Note: Most unusually large group is shown when each place is compared with the UK, in the
case of conflicts, then the following household types which appear first in this order got priority:
Married (with children), Married (children returned), Married (no children), Other (with children),
Lone parent, Cohabiting couple (no children), Lone pensioner, Lone adult, Student, Pensioner,
Mixed.

Source: Analysis of the 2001 Census Key Statistics by local authority.

Next, Figure 4.7 shows one version of the within-Britain migration picture, not just for children but for people of all ages, using the same technique that has been used throughout this chapter, of labelling places according to the group from one of the census Key Statistics tables which is most in excess in the area compared to its numbers nationally.

Figure 4.7 Migration in England and Wales, 2000–2001

Note: Most unusually large group is shown when each place is compared with England and Wales.

Source: Analysis of the 2001 Census Key Statistics by local authority.

The groups used in Figure 4.7 are not mutually exclusive and exhaustive. People can be (and are) both in-migrants and out-migrants between areas simultaneously. This data was not included in the Northern Irish and Scottish Key Statistics. In England and Wales the most common label is that a place is typified by people who don't tend to move house. These are the suburbs and, just a little further out of town, the ex-urbs where families settle for years. Next most common are places where people tend only to move locally if they do move, swapping houses for an extra bedroom or a 'better area'. Almost equal are the last and smallest two categories: areas where an unusual number move in from outside the local district (these form a ring around London) and the areas they move from (London), often at the cost of their time in much more commuting.

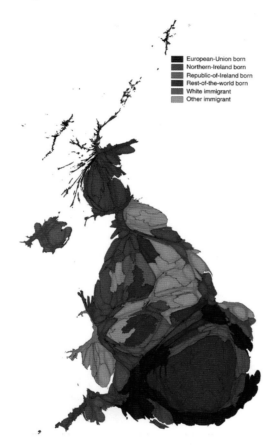

European-Union born
Northern-Ireland born
Republic-of-Ireland born
Rest-of-the-world born
White immigrant
Other immigrant

Figure 4.8 Lifetime and annual immigration to the UK by 2001

Note: Most unusually large group is shown when each place is compared with the UK. All immigrants since 2000 are labelled either White or Other Immigrant.

Source: Analysis of the 2001 Census Key Statistics by local authority.

What, though, of people who move into and out of Britain? The accuracy of the 2001 census was largely based on a quite well-informed guess that at least a million more people left these shores in the late 1990s than we first thought had. These were people who had left before 2001, before the counting of who was here in 2001 had begun. For those coming in we have a much better idea of their origins and locations. Figure 4.8 stretches the method used so far in this chapter even further by combining overlapping statistics from two tables: one of where people were born (if overseas) and their ethnicity (if recent arrivals). The figure can be characterised as describing a series of rings of immigration, past and present, which radiate out from London.

In Figure 4.8 London is typified as being wholly made up of, and largely housing, unusually high numbers (for Britain) of people born outside the European Union (EU) – 'Rest-of-the-World born'. Surrounding it is a ring of areas of people born in the EU (excluding Britain and Ireland), broken only by areas to which Irish-born immigrants have moved since settling in Britain many years ago. Above them in 2001 was a northern and Welsh band of areas labelled 'Other immigrant'. These are places where, often resettled from London, there were higher than usual numbers of then non-White arrivals.

Figure 4.9 Highest level of qualification gained by people in the UK, 2001

Note: Most unusually large group is shown when each place is compared with the UK.

Source: Analysis of the 2001 Census Key Statistics by local authority.

Above those areas and in a scattering of other places, Northern Ireland emigrants dominated as being the most likely immigrant group. The 'Other immigrant' belt was partly made up of people who had recently arrived in these countries, often fleeing persecution in poor countries or wars (many of which we were partly involved in), and who had been settled in these more peripheral places by the authorities.

What do people come to Britain for? Many come to work, but others come – and often pay dearly – for education, particularly university education. Just as within Britain, access to a university determines many life chances, so too worldwide. This, however, is just a very small part of the explanation for the pattern of identity shown in Figure 4.9, the pattern that this book began trying to explain in Chapter 1, the pattern that the movement of children described in Chapter 2 results from, and the pattern that is partly the result of the education system described in Chapter 3 – the pattern of that part of people's identities formed through their qualifications.

The 2001 census was the first census to ask everyone about their qualifications, not just those with university degrees. What it revealed showed why education matters so much (for the sorting of children much more than for learning and teaching). If you have any doubt that education plays the major part in deciding where you end up living, just spend a minute looking at Figure 4.9 of the population with university degrees. There are, of course, people with degrees living in every area of Britain (their numbers are given in Figure 3.9), but within each area the pattern of location is as segregated as that shown nationally here. The UK is a set of nations sharply divided by what passes for acquired knowledge.

The geographical link between the last figure and the final form of identity shown in this chapter (in Figure 4.10) does not require a great leap of imagination. Social class is the form of identity that in many ways social science began with. Classes are constantly defined and redefined and a new classification system was used in the 2001 census Key Statistics, but no matter how they alter the definitions, the basic pattern prevails. People with no social class (under the new system which was envisaged to give everyone a class!) include those who have not worked recently: pensioners, many lone parents, people retired on grounds of ill health and so on.

What is most interesting about Figure 4.10 is not the extent to which it confirms our prejudices but what it tells us which might be new and might be the beginning of some major change. Consider, for example, the relative geographic isolation of the seven areas with unusual numbers working on their own account (only a minority will be farmers). And why is the only area with a preponderance of the highest class – managers – Cheshire East? Do the modern equivalent of mill owners need to crowd together for safety in the North? Why is one area of London typified by people who have never worked and where 165,000 people have degrees? See Figure 4.3, above, for what might be part of the answer. Almost everyone who has never worked is a young adult.

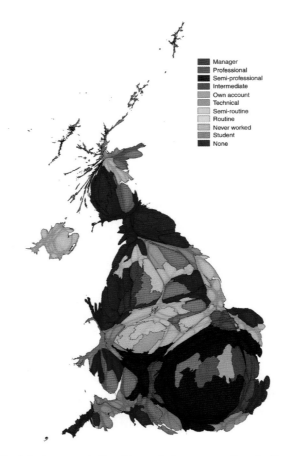

Manager
Professional
Semi-professional
Intermediate
Own account
Technical
Semi-routine
Routine
Never worked
Student
None

Figure 4.10 Social class as defined largely by occupation in the UK, 2001

Note: Most unusually large group is shown when each place is compared with the UK.

Source: Analysis of the 2001 Census Key Statistics by local authority.

AN EXERCISE

(Preferably 84 players, but can be played with 336, 252, 168, 42, 21 or 10 and numbers in between with some careful organisation).

Before you begin, assign each player to one of the 84 areas of Britain. If you have more than 84 players, work in groups. If you have fewer, each player is responsible for more than one area or, more easily, you could use only part of Britain. The instructions here are written assuming that you have exactly 84 players but it is not difficult to adapt them. Northern Ireland is excluded here because it has no clear neighbour in the rest of the UK.

1 Each player needs to construct the hypothetical atypical individual living in
   their area using the information contained in Figures 4.1–4.10. If that place
   were a person, who would that person be? Note: this person is not typical of
   the area and may not even exist. Instead, they are typical about what is
   atypical of their area, what identities are more clustered there than in other
   places. For example, here is the atypical occupant of London Central:

4.1 Female

4.2 Aged 25–29

4.3 Black African

4.4 Muslim

4.5 Single

4.6 Living alone

4.7 Many neighbours left the area since last year

4.8 Born outside the EU

4.9 Has a university degree or equivalent

4.10 Professional occupation

---

2 Once the players have defined their identities they need to move around the
   room or lecture theatre so that their 84 bodies are arranged as the map of
   Britain has been arranged in the Figures 4.1–4.10. They should have several
   neighbours. Identify each neighbour corresponding to the area immediately
   around you. Again you have formed a map of Britain.

3 Next compare your identities to those of your neighbours. On how many
   of the ten do you differ? For instance, to the east of the person who is
   London Central is London East and they differ on seven identities marked*
   below:

4.1 Female

4.2 Aged 0–4*

4.3 Indian*

4.4 Muslim (parents)

4.5 Married (parents)*

                                              (Continued)

(Continued)

   4.6 Married with kid(s)*

   4.7 People tend not to move home in the area*

   4.8 Born outside the EU

   4.9 Parents have no qualifications*

   4.10 Intermediate occupation*

4 Now move slightly away from the neighbour(s) you share least in common with and slightly towards those who are most similar to you. Someone looking down on the room from above should see a geographical map of social and cultural divides and similarities opening up before their eyes.

5 To find where the greatest local divides in the UK are, someone needs to call out numbers: 'Is there any pair of people in the room who differ on all ten identities? On nine? How many on eight?' and so on. Where are these divides and is a pattern beginning to form to connect them? Are any two neighbouring areas identical in their identities? Are any pairs of non-neighbour areas identical in their identities?

6 Finally, start with the greatest local divides identified above and attempt to connect them using the next greatest adjacent divides to eventually divide the room and yourselves into two roughly equally sized groups. Your dividing line should ideally be continuous. It may become quite convoluted and complex as you attempt to link enclaves and exclude pockets that do not fit their original side of the line. It is advisable, and mildly amusing, to use a ball of wool to construct this line, starting with the pair of individuals who have least in common holding the wool in the middle and sending both ends out either way from between them to attempt to eventually join those two ends together again, having split the UK in two.

With over 84 players it may be advisable not to attempt this last part of the exercise, especially if anyone needs to use the toilet in the near future.

If you are wondering what the purpose of the exercise is, it is to dispel a myth. It is often said by eminent social researchers that it is not possible to define areas as being rich or poor and to then expect them to contain most rich or poor people within them (or any other two groups). This is not true. It is possible. It is just that the dividing line you might have to construct, to be perfect, would be very long and very complex. It would snake up one street, taking in the odd house or two, then encompass an entire estate, save for a single person living in a flat in the middle, for whom a special loop would have to be drawn. The line would appear fractal in shape, like a coastline but even more convoluted than that.

Such lines are drawn every day in the world. Rather like geo-demographics, there is a small industry that has developed to draw them. Political maps and voting districts are constantly redrawn, often in the interests of a particular group or party. This is known as 'gerrymandering', particularly where the attempt is to draw lines around voters to win seats. The job of gerrymanderers can be even more complex than yours when they try to draw lines around groups of people who are different from one another to ensure that the group they favour is just larger than the group they do not like; but more on them in the next chapter.

Finally, having geographically divided the UK into two halves, compare the differences between areas either side of the dividing line to the differences between areas on the edge of one half and in its centre. Do areas either side of the line have more in common with each other than they do with other areas in their half? If so, what maintains the line of the line?

Conclusion

I have done what this chapter began by criticising. I have labelled places in ways that it can easily be argued are arbitrary. I have used a consistent method, but had I used different areas, different labels or different statistics about the same labels, the pictures would be a little different. Labelling is never precise. Places are mixtures as much as people are mixtures. Some men behave more like most women, some 30-year-olds behave like, or have the health of, a 40-year-old.

They say you are as young or as old as you feel! We are all a mixture of ethnicities, of origins. This is most true for people labelled 'White', whose ancestors are likely to have come from a wide range of areas, cultures, religions and to have spoken many languages – simply because rates of migration within Europe and from elsewhere were so high in the last few hundred years. Few of us believe in a single, simply defined god that is simply 'god'. We all have our own beliefs and no two will quite match up. And yet people are willing to tick a box labelled 'religion'. Similarly, people who did not tick the box did not for a wide variety of reasons.

On a personal note, the religion (Jedi) I entered and defended in the newspapers (using the pseudonym L. Skywalker) was not recognised as a religious group despite outnumbering Sikhs, Jews and Buddhists on the census forms. If the census authorities don't like your answer, they delete it, as they did for gay people in 1991 and for many other groups before that. People are not simply single, married, divorced or widowed. The addition of remarried, and married but separated, to the latest census began to address this, but happily married, unhappily married, having an affair, two-timing my girlfriend, happy at home with the cats or living in a *ménage-à-trois* and endless other possibilities are all negated by labelling. Categorising people by households also does this.

Being a pensioner living alone with no family can be very different from being a pensioner living alone in the house next door to your grown-up child. Similarly, we are all migrants and immigrants of different kinds, and we all have qualifications, most of which are not measured and for which you do not receive certificates. For instance, I cannot easily spell words over five letters long, but there was no box on the census form to let them know this. Finally, class is not a single simple ten-fold division of the population. There are a myriad of facets to class. You don't either have the attributes of a class or not. All jobs are 'semi-routine', some just pay much better than others, involve a great deal more freedom and allow you to lord (a gendered expression note!) it over others more.

Why label then? One answer is that without labelling we could not begin to understand how the world works and, most importantly, because there is a little truth in the labels. Men do, on average, behave differently from women. This is a very large part of the reason why men are more likely to die a bit younger. Class matters throughout your life – and through into the lives of your children and their children until the underlying social structure changes.

People are killed for believing in particular religions. People are treated very differently according to their skin colour (and again in Britain are occasionally killed because of it). Labels matter. As long as we realise the damage they can do, the arbitrariness of their imposition and their intangibility and ephemerality, then we should use them. We have little choice. Everything, after all, is a label. For instance, each and every one of these words is one. You are labelling me as you read this 'bleeding heart, opinionated, liberal academic who doesn't know when to use only one word when he's given the space to use ten'! But how many labels to use and when to stop labelling …?

I could have written hundreds of pages on each map and for each map I could have drawn another hundred maps and written another hundred pages on each of them. However, as each additional map was drawn there would be less and less of substance to say. There is a simple, crude, true, describable, explainable, human geography to Britain. The majority of that quantitative picture is shown in the ten maps drawn in this chapter. After this, diminishing returns set in.

The simple form of labelling used here is no cruder than any other, just more explicit. The patterns that you have just seen are the patterns that underlie almost all other maps of people's lives in these countries – they are influenced by them and influence them in turn. Only 60 or so million people live here. Less than a percentage of the world's population and, proportionately, falling. Britain is a small island and by far the most mapped island in the world. If we could not say with some certainty what people were doing, who they were, why they were here and where they are going, we could do so nowhere else on earth. Before you dismiss this form of stereotyping think about your life, the life of your fellow students and why you are all in the same room together. Ask your tutor where they came from. Will they not tell you? If so, why not? Perhaps it's because it will tell you a little too much about them?

Further Reading

The Geodemographics industry is large and getting larger all the time. One of the sayings of the industry is 'If we know where you live, then we know who you are'. In Britain one of the largest companies is called Experian. According to the Market Research Society's listing of information about this company, 'Experian's Business Strategies Division provides a detailed understanding and analysis of consumers, markets and economies in the UK and around the world. Its focus is consumer profiling and market segmentation, retail property analysis, economic forecasting and public policy research. The division is responsible for the creation of the MOSAIC household-level geodemographic classification which is available in 25 countries and classifies more than a million consumers worldwide' (see www.geodemographics.org.uk/datasources.html). Why not try to find out what Experian records about you and your family? The office of the Information Commissioner has been set up to give advice to individuals about openness and privacy (see www.ico.gov.uk).

Key Point Summary

- Different areas of the UK can be typified as having particular groupings of people.

- The elderly move towards the edges; people with qualifications tend to drift south.

- The labelling of areas can both helpfully illuminate and harmfully stereotype.

5

POLITICS

... counting democracy, wasting votes

People are labelled by where they live using a variety of sources far wider than the census and they are, of course, themselves responsible for some of the labelling. In most cases, however, it is just a very small group of people who construct the labels through which much of our lives are described. In Britain these very small groups claim legitimacy in their labelling because either they are directly empowered to label others through the democratic process or the democratic process defends their rights to label.

Democratically elected government defends and helps assert the rights of private companies, in a free market, to label populations by where they live. Similarly, researchers working in universities are both protected and encouraged by government to take part in such work, while many civil servants are directly employed by government to label places, most obviously through the construction of the decennial census and the analysis of what it can reveal.

The labelling of places is part of democratically elected government in many ways. It enables government to target resources, for instance, or to see to what extent the nations it commands are moving apart or coming together. However, the same techniques that can be used to label places can also be used to examine how democratically elected governments come to be in power; to discern who votes for them, where their votes come from, how effective those votes are in returning their members to government, to see who is not voting or voting for other parties and how that is changing.

The labelling of places is used to help put into power those who sanction and fund much of that labelling. It has long been argued that government needs to know, in detail, the characteristics of the populations it governs in order to govern them, in its terms, effectively. Over time, surveillance of the population tends to increase. The fact that government also needs to know these characteristics to ensure that it is elected to govern is less widely appreciated.

In this chapter the geographical patterns of voting and political representation resulting from the British general election of 2010 are briefly described and compared to the earlier 2001 election. The earlier election was held just a few weeks after the census of that year. The two had to be seen to be independent so the census was not delayed despite the quarantine of many countryside areas due to the foot-and-mouth outbreak in cattle and sheep. There was much speculation that the government's handling of that outbreak would affect its pattern of votes and hence its majority in parliament, but in the event hardly any effect could be seen at all.

The 2001 election returned the governing Labour party to power with a majority hardly altered from that which it had achieved in its landslide victory four years earlier; little appeared to have changed in those four years. In fact, when the geographical patterns are considered a great deal was found to have altered. The bias in voting had increased. It took fewer votes to elect each Labour MP in 2001 as compared to 1997 because the Labour vote became more efficiently distributed in terms of maximising the number of MPs elected. You would have to look at Chapter 5 of the first edition of this book (published in 2005 under the title *Human Geography of the UK*) to read about that, as the world has moved on and we have more recent elections to consider now. Also note that voting bias fell after 2001.

In 1997, with 32% of the electorate voting for it, Labour won 65% of the mainland Westminster parliamentary constituencies. In 2001, with the support of 25% of the electorate, it won 64% of those constituencies. In 2005, despite its support falling to just 22% of the electorate, it still won 55% of those mainland seats. There were too few in Northern Ireland, just 3% of all seats, to threaten that majority and so, despite losing almost one-third of their support between 1997 and 2005 and losing the vote of one in ten adults in Britain, Labour carried on holding power with an absolute majority in the House of Commons, but even a slight continuation of that trend was destined to cast Labour out of power.

In 2010, with only 19% of voters remaining loyal to Labour, its share of Westminster constituencies fell to 41% and the Labour party could no longer command an absolute majority in the House of Commons. Their major opponent, the Conservative party, had secured 24% of the support of electorate, but their vote was far more inefficiently arranged around the UK than Labour's had been, and that support won them only 48% of mainland seats; too few to form a majority even with the help of Unionist Northern Irish MPs, their traditional allies. Parliament was hung and a coalition with the Liberals was formed.

Figure 5.1 shows the proportion of Conservative and Liberal MPs elected into power in each area of Britain. The European constituencies tend to be made up of either seven or eight Westminster constituencies (or 'seats'). Elections to the Westminster parliament are held on a first-past-the-post basis, where the candidate winning most votes in a seat wins that seat and the other votes are wasted. As should be evident from the numbers in the discussion above, this is the most biased system of all the different electoral systems used in Britain, which a cynic may see as appropriate since it is that which elects representatives to the most powerful political body.

Between them in 2010, the major two parties (Labour and Conservatives) secured the support of only 43% of the electorate (19% + 24%) and yet were awarded 90% of the Westminster constituencies (if the Speaker's seat is included). The main reason for this is that 35% of the electorate chose not to vote, often because their vote would be pointless, but also because people started voting more for what were previously minor parties. Many could see little difference between the people they were being asked to choose between, especially between those who had a chance of winning. However, when given the chance to vote in a referendum in 2011 on changing the voting system, most who voted chose to keep the old system. It later turned out that the campaign group arguing for no change had received the most funding, especially funding from a few very wealthy donors.

In large parts of the North, Scotland and Wales, entire European constituencies are only represented by Labour MPs. In 2001 only in four areas of the South were there places not represented by Labour MPs. By 2010, as Figure 5.1 reveals, there were at least 20 such areas. Of course, many people in the former areas did not vote Labour and quite a few people in the latter areas did vote for Labour. These people's democratically expressed wishes were ignored in the

Figure 5.1 Conservative and Liberal candidates elected as MPs in Britain, 2010

Source: Analysis of the 2010 general election results, proportion of Conservative and Liberal candidates per European constituency elected to a Westminster constituency.

selection of MPs for Westminster. The first question to ask of the map in Figure 5.1 is to what extent does the geography of political representation reflect the geography of political desires, and how has that changed since 2001?

In 2001, in each European constituency between 11% and 36% of the electorate (those eligible to vote) voted for Labour, a very small (or at most a small-ish) minority in every case. In Northern Ireland no one voted Labour because they were not presented with that choice. The most pernicious bias in the British electoral system is the limitation of effective choice given by the very small number of candidates presented to each elector. Very few voters are presented with an option to vote for a truly socialist candidate, for instance. Only in one constituency can a vote for the Green party result in a Green MP being elected.

In 2010 in each European constituency between 12% and 60% of the electorate voted either Liberal or Conservative. Figure 5.2 highlights the minority

Figure 5.2 Proportion of electorate voting Conservative or Liberal in Britain, 2010

Source: Analysis of the 2010 general election results, proportion of Conservative or Liberal votes per European constituency of all people eligible to vote.

of areas which did give majority support for these two parties. However, voting in that part of the map was so high for them because they were mostly opposing each other there! Cynicism is likely to rise further. In 2001, nationally, Labour won 25% of the electorate, 42% of the vote, and 64% of the seats in Britain. In 2010, nationally, the Conservatives won 24% of the electorate, 37% of the vote, and 49% of the seats, but their leader became Prime Minister despite that.

Proportionately, for every 1% of the electorate who voted for the Labour party, that party won 2.6% of the seats in the 2001 general election. In 2010 the Conservatives won 2.0% of seats for every 1.0% of the electorate. The first-past-the-post electoral system tends to award winners disproportionately in this way, but the disproportionality is far from geographically even. Figure 5.3 shows why the Conservatives in 2010 did not do nearly as well as Labour in

Figure 5.3   Conservative vote, increase in share of electorate in Britain, 2001–2010

Source: Analysis of the 2001 and 2010 general election results, per European constituency.

2001 despite having an almost equal electorate share. In short, the Conservatives increased their support most where it had been strongest to begin with: in (what was for them) the wrong places.

The greatest rise in Conservative support between the general elections of 2001 and 2010 was in the constituencies of the Thames Valley, where an additional 11% of the electorate chose to support them over this period. By 2010 half the electorate voted for the Conservatives or Liberals here, just one-seventh for Labour, but the Labour vote was concentrated in the Westminster constituency of Slough and so a single Labour MP was still returned in 2010. It was because the Conservatives were not as good as Labour had been at encouraging people in the right places to vote for them that they failed to secure an outright majority of Westminster seats in 2010. The Liberals did even worse. They lost seats in aggregate between the general elections of 2005 and 2010. In particular, two of the Thames Valley seats they had held in 2001 had become Conservative seats by 2010. Yet they still entered government in 2010 because of the hung parliament.

To show how much geography does matter, and what the Conservatives failed to achieve in 2010, consider Figure 5.4. In 1997 Labour won the support in Britain of 32% of the electorate and secured 65% of the seats; in 2001 they won the support of only 25% of the electorate but 64% of the seats. Their vote-to-seats ratio rose from 2.06 to 2.59 (in 1997 they won just over twice as high a share of seats as compared to their share of votes, 65/32 = 2.06, by 2001 that ratio had risen to 64/25 = 2.59). Each vote for Labour was far more effective when cast just four years later, but that pattern was not evenly spread across the UK, as Figure 5.4 shows. In a few areas the effectiveness of a Labour vote fell slightly, but that was rare. Effectiveness is the ratio of the proportion of seats to votes, and it is the change in that ratio that is mapped in Figure 5.4. Generally, the further north and west you travelled in 2001, the more effective a vote for Labour became.

In 2001 only one-quarter of the population eligible to vote voted for the party which secured almost two-thirds of the seats. Every vote is equal, but some votes, most importantly those for Labour away from the South East (outside London), were very much more equal than others and were becoming more so. How did we get to the situation of electing a government, both in 2001 and 2010, which was supported by so few, and even those few having so little choice over which party to support? In most Labour seats only Labour can win. In most cases where the seat is marginal the only other party which can win are the Conservatives. In most Conservative seats only the Conservatives can win. This is not a great deal of choice, and is hardly increased by the Liberal Democrats, and then in only a few places, and then they could easily join the party you might not have voted for once they are in power!

It would be very wrong to assume that support for the Labour party was highest in 2001 in the North and West of Britain and London. Figure 5.5 illustrates how that support was highest there for no party (this remains the case today).

■	≥ 0.8
■	0.6 to 0.8
▦	0.4 to 0.6
▨	0.2 to 0.4
□	0 to 0.2
▨	0 and below
▨	no data

Figure 5.4   Change in bias towards Labour, 1997–2001

Note: No change is 0; a change of 1 implies an extra 1% MPs per 1% vote.

Source: Analysis of the 1997 and 2001 election results.

In fact, a majority of electors in six areas shown in Figure 5.5 did not vote for any party. Nationally, 41% of electors did not vote in 2001 as compared to 28% just four years earlier. Some 39% did not vote in 2005 and 35% did not vote in 2010. Of those who did vote in 2010, a record 6% voted for a party other than the main three.

Above all else, it was the rise in abstentions from 1997–2001 that accounted for the rise in bias that made every remaining vote for Labour so much more valuable, but also made the political arithmetic so precarious. A majority of the electorate in 2001, as measured by first-past-the-post (or at least the single largest group as measured conventionally), chose to support no political party, and this was the case everywhere and for all other political parties at the level of geography used throughout this book. Political bias is high because a growing number of people do not want to choose between what they are offered. They see so little point in the process. That was the case in 2001 and remains the case in 2010 other than in the West of Scotland, where rising support for the Nationalists reduced abstentions and meant that a higher proportion voted Labour than abstained in 2010. Political arithmetic can get convoluted.

Figure 5.5 Proportion of the electorate abstaining in Britain, 2010

Source: Analysis of the 2010 general election results, proportion of Westminster electorate not voting per European constituency.

It was after 1997 that apathy rose as disillusionment set in. The proportion of the electorate who chose not to vote increased everywhere between 1997 and 2001; it increased most in the North West of England and in Scotland, where it was already very high. Figure 5.6 shows the rise in abstentions over the entire 1997–2010 period. Initially rising abstentions, given that they required the government to secure fewer votes for victory, were in the interest of the Parliamentary Labour Party in terms of securing the continued dominance of its government. But by 2010 the falling away of Labour support was too much.

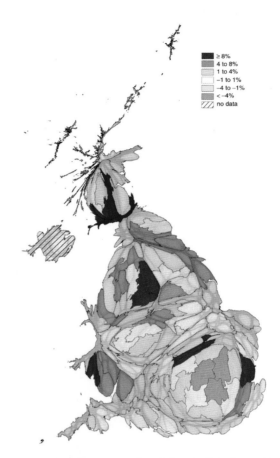

Figure 5.6   Increase in the electorate abstaining in Britain, 1997–2010

Source: Analysis of the 1997 and 2010 general election results, rise (and decline) in the proportion of Westminster electorate not voting per European constituency between the elections of
1997 and 2010.

Abstentions were reduced the most in central London and Sheffield where
many people fought hard in the few marginal areas to defend Labour seats. They
succeeded in preventing a Conservative majority. Abstentions rose least or fell
slightly in those places where voters were most opposed to the Labour party and
tried to use their votes to express this. Many there realised how the electoral system worked, and understood how futile such an attempt was before 2010. In the
run-up to a general election the electorate is bombarded with information suggesting that its vote counts immensely. Almost nothing is said about some people's
votes counting much more than others and many being of no consequence at all.
Overall, despite this lack of information, more and more electors would appear to
realise that for them, individually, voting may usually be futile, although that feeling diminishes somewhat when it appears a parliament may be hung.

Why vote at all if your vote carries so little weight when you don't vote for the ruling party? One answer is because it has not always been, and will not always be, like it is today. In 1997 the electorate of Britain voted out a Conservative government which had been in power for 18 years. There are many reasons as to why voters did this, but it is important to realise that popularity does not necessarily lead to power. For instance, in 1951 a majority of the electorate voted Labour but they won a minority of the seats. In 1997 the electorate voted both strongly and effectively for Labour. They voted most strongly, as they have always done, in those areas which are most disadvantaged by how life in Britain is organised.

One example of the connections between social advantage, disadvantage and voting is the education system, which is largely run by government. Figure 5.7 compares the proportion of children who achieved low qualifications at school before and just after the 1997 general election with the proportion of adults (including many of these children's parents) who voted for Labour in 1997. The Labour party, being the party that historically arose from the people who benefited least from the state, was the political party seen in 1997 as being most likely

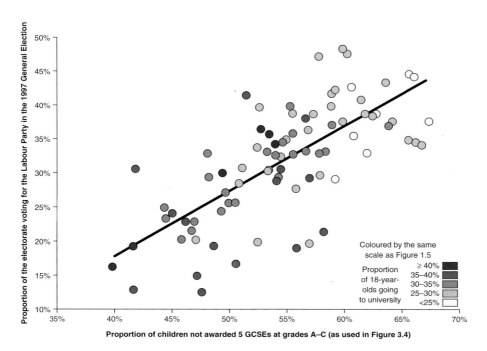

Figure 5.7 Voting Labour in 1997 versus low qualifications, 1993–99

Note: Coloured by the same scale as Figures 1.5, 1.7, 2.4 and 2.9 to allow comparison with those maps and diagrams.

Source: Analysis of national school league tables for Britain 1993–99; general election data 1997, available online, e.g. from the UK Electoral Commission.

to rectify this injustice (among many other injustices). 'Education, education, education' was one of the political slogans of that party. The circles in the figure are shaded by chance of going to university, which indicates that this is not simple to predict from the average area rate of failure at age 16. Many young people, especially in London, do well in areas where others do badly, especially around age 18 rather than 16.

The Labour government, first elected to power in 1997, may well have helped improve the education system, or at least have stopped it becoming as unequal as it might have become, along with many other aspects of society. However, that government also failed to convince many of its supporters that it was doing so, which is part of the reason why its support fell so fast among the electorate. The electoral system and its particular geographical distribution of votes initially prevented that decline in support having any real effect. Figure 5.7 shows part of the reason why so many people in poorer areas voted Labour. Their children tended to do worse at school, and Labour appeared to be the party most likely to change that. As earlier chapters have indicated, the evidence to date suggests that Labour did reduce the education gap a little, but most of the evidence that it did do was revealed only after May 2010.

Why should many of the electorate perceive a government as not delivering, for example on education? One reason is that it is not easy to change a great deal in a short space of time. Another reason is that the impetus for change among MPs may not be too great. It is perhaps unsurprising that MPs might not see educational disadvantage as being really the most pressing of problems. Most of them have benefited from such disadvantage. Figure 5.8 shows the proportion of MPs elected to a seat in 2001 in each area who were educated in what appears to have been a comprehensive, secondary modern, or other generally non-selective state-funded school.

In a majority of areas only one or no MPs out of the seven or eight representing the constituencies therein were educated as the majority of their constituents were. Only in ten areas were more than 50% of MPs so educated. Two-thirds of children were, and still are now, taught in non-selective state schools (Figure 3.5). Less than one-third (177) of the MPs who represented them and their parents had similar backgrounds. Admittedly, 150 of those 177 were Labour MPs, but that was still only 36% of the parliamentary Labour representation. It is also fair to say that most MPs were educated when the 11-plus was in place, but few younger Members of Parliament have not been to university. MPs tend to have more in common with each other than with their constituencies and, as time passes and MPs' salaries rise, this becomes ever more the case. Today there are far fewer Labour MPs in office and so even fewer MPs in the House of Commons with similar backgrounds to most of their electors.

General elections are a remarkably good mechanism for annoying voters. Even after ignoring the largest single group of electors – those who chose not to vote – in 2001 there remained almost a majority of people who voted but who did not see the candidate they voted for win, some 12.5 million voters

Figure 5.8   MPs educated in non-selective state schools, 2001

Note: Figure relies on data of variable quality.

Source: Short bibliographies of MPs and candidates published in various guides to the general election.

or 49% of everyone who voted (Figure 5.9 shows how little this varied across the UK). Only 8.3 million or 32% of all voters voted for the Labour party and saw their candidate win in 2001. That leaves 68% of everyone who voted either seeing their preferred candidate lose, or seeing their preferred candidate win but the party in question fail to form a government (and so their elected representative has very little real power).

Other than in the United States of America, where the choice is only ever between two parties, it is difficult to think of a supposedly democratic electoral mechanism better designed to annoy large numbers of the electorate most of the time. Remember also that many of the 8.3 million people who voted Labour and saw their candidate win may well have done so since they saw the Labour candidate as the least worst alternative. In practice, less than one-tenth of the entire population of Britain may actually be getting what they really want when it comes to democracy in these countries. And that situation is getting worse.

≥ 60%	
55 to 60%	
50 to 55%	
45 to 50%	
< 45%	
no data	

Figure 5.9   Proportion of the voters not having their wish honoured, 2001

Source: Analysis of the 2010 general election results percentage of voters in each area voting for a candidate who did not win a seat in that area.

The final map in this chapter, Figure 5.10, shows the proportion of voters who did not have their wishes expressed through political representation when they voted in 2010. By now the proportion who voted, but who did not see the person they voted for win, had risen to 53%; a majority! This was partly because the votes had become a little more evenly shared between the three main parties, but also because more people were now voting for minor parties than had ever done so before.

Only in five places in Scotland and the North West of England did between 52% and 57% of voters see their wishes acted upon. In these places a majority of those who voted had voted Labour in 2010, but of course they did not see a single one of their representatives enter government (just parliament). In 12 places, almost encircling central London, a narrow majority of between 50.3% and 55% did see the candidate they voted for become MP, but again some will have not seen that MP enter government and even more will have tactically voted for a Liberal candidate to try to prevent a Conservative administration and then have unwittingly aided one coming to power as their Liberal MP entered parliament in coalition.

Figure 5.10 Proportion of voters not having their wish honoured, 2010

Source: Analysis of the 2010 general election results by European constituency.

Britain has one of the strangest of parliamentary democracies where rising numbers of people who vote do not get what they voted for and yet the electorate can be encouraged to vote in favour of such a system simply by being told it is in their interest and believing the people with most money who tell them this (see Further Reading below). How high do you think the numbers in Figure 5.10 could go before it is no longer sensible to describe the system as democratic?

AN EXERCISE

First-past-the-post elections are very easy to understand, or at least they appear to be. As the maps above have shown, it is much harder to understand what they result in or why there are particular patterns as to who does not get what they wish for despite voting, than it is to understand the voting system. Under the Westminster first-past-the-post system anyone who is over 18 and not in an excluded category can stand as an MP provided that they can find enough money to pay the deposit required (which they lose if they secure less than 5% of the vote). They also need to be able to take the time off work or childcare to campaign, so most people are excluded. However, they only have a chance of winning if they are selected by one of the two or three main parties in an area, and usually it is just one party whose candidate has any chance of winning so the votes don't count; what matters is winning the party selection process.

Here is how to play *'Who wants to be a member of parliament?'*:

1   Each player, each person in the class, needs to choose a persona from having carried out the exercise at the end of Chapter 4. The quick way to do this is to pick a number from 1 to 64 at random. To do this you start with the number 1. Toss a coin, if it is heads add 1; do it again, if heads add 2; again add 4; again add 8; again add 16; again add 32. At each point if it is tails add nothing. Use that number to select one of the English European constituencies from 1 to 64. Suppose you tossed only tails. Your number would be 1 and your constituency would be London central. Your characteristics would then be:

Female

Aged 25–29

Black African

Muslim

Single

Living alone

Many neighbours left the area since last year

Born outside the European Union

Has a university degree or equivalent

Professional occupation

---

2   Each person then needs to decide for which political party group they want to be an MP. It might be wise to pick a party that you think might be more sympathetic to someone from your background. Choose between the three

main parties, Conservative, Labour and Liberal Democrat, and get into groups (by political party). If you cannot choose between these three you can join a fourth group called 'most voters'.

3 Within each group you need to pick a single candidate. The following instructions tell you how to do this. If you are in the 'most voters' group, then simply chat about the weather or what happens to be interesting you today. Whatever you do, *don't* talk about politics as you are representative of most people and most people don't do this.

4 If you are within one of the main party groups, each of you decide whether you need to rule yourselves out. For instance, you must be a British, Irish or Commonwealth country citizen to stand; you must also think you have the time and the personality needed.

5 All those not standing within each party make up the selection committee. You need to interview each candidate in turn, ask them about their background, whether any of it is relevant to their candidature and how the skills they have might be useful in getting them elected. When all have been interviewed, vote for a winner.

6 If you are within the 'most voters', group carry on talking about the weather, where you would like to go on holiday or if you can afford to go on holiday, what you hope for the future and who is to blame for things not being as you might wish (but don't mention politics).

7 If you are within one of the three party groups, the time has come to hold an election. If you are the Liberal candidate, you have lost. That is what happens to almost all Liberal candidates. Pick another random number from 1 to 64 and then look at how the votes are normally distributed in that area using Figure 5.1. If normally more than 60% of the seats are won by the coalition, then the Conservative candidate is duly elected. If less than 40% normally go to the coalition, then the Labour candidate is elected. Otherwise, if the proportion is between 40% and 60%, go to step 8 below.

8 If you happen to have chosen somewhere where the result is not likely to be a foregone conclusion, then you need to involve the 'most voters group'. Whichever of the two main candidates' parties has the most money in their pockets is allowed the most time to convince the 'most voters group' to vote for them. Share out 60 seconds in proportion to how much money both parties have. This is called 'campaigning'. Good luck (although luck doesn't have a great deal to do with it).

Conclusion

This is not a fanciful game. It is played out constantly in the UK, which, unlike most democratic countries, still runs an arcane system of voting that ensures that most people's votes don't matter and when they do matter, whichever party can dig deepest into the pockets of its donors can gain a great advantage in securing the most seats. Of course people get bored of parties over time and so they tend to swing between them, blaming the party that has been in power the longest for their woes rather than the system that put them there and which makes it so hard for people to behave well.

In the first edition of this book, this chapter ended with a different and very complex exercise to try to explain how constituency boundaries were altered over time. However, some of the rules for making such alterations were torn up by the incoming coalition government of May 2010. You see, whoever gains power in Britain is allowed to do largely as they like. I tried to explain back then that under the unwritten rules Westminster Constituencies in Britain cannot cross county boundaries; must be almost equal in population size, all in the name of periodic boundary change.

Most difficult of all, I tried to explain how, under the official rules of the actual game in the UK, you cannot admit that you are playing this game or that there are great problems with UK voting systems and constituency boundary reorganisations. Instead you have to suggest that ward X should be moved into constituency Y because it has long-standing historical links with that area ever since farmer Z first took his cart to market in Y in 1066. Furthermore, you have to contend with a huge number of local mavericks who have their own particular interest in just one boundary or another.

It is rather like playing the game of Mornington Crescent (which used to be aired on the establishment channel, BBC Radio 4). You are not allowed to admit you know what the rules are. And, just like Mornington Crescent, most people do not realise what the rules really are – they are just very complex and secret. The worst thing you could do would be to try to claim there were no rules. That would be similar to suggesting that the UK had no written and understandable constitution …

Further Reading

If you are interested in who the financial traders, stockbrokers and former bank bosses were who mostly funded the campaign against changing the electoral system in May 2011, then see the *Guardian* newspaper story at www.guardian. co.uk/politics/2011/may/03/av-referendum-details-donations-yes-no-campaigns, which also documents how the 'Yes' campaign managed to lose despite appearing to have received almost a million more pounds in funding than the 'No' campaign. However, by the November of 2011 it was revealed that the campaign funding had been the other way round, with a million more pounds being spent on the 'No' campaign. All these details were revealed by the on-line *Huffington Post*: www.huffingtonpost.co.uk/2011/11/29/no-to-av-campaign-outspent-rival-yes-camp-by-1m_n_1118164.html.

Compare these reports on voting and campaign spending in Britain with two BBC stories on voting in China. China doesn't have as large financial penalties to prevent people from standing (although it does have many more political prisoners): 'Voters in China's local elections are allowed to cast their vote for their own candidate by writing its name under the official lists of candidates on the ballot paper' (see www.bbc.co.uk/news/world-asia-china-15649473 from 9 November 2011) and 'Four of the six candidates were voted in, including the non-Party member' (see news.bbc.co.uk/1/shared/spl/hi/picture_gallery/06/ programmes_china0s_village_ballot_box/html/10.stm from 13 June 2006). Are the political systems of Britain and China really as different as they are so often portrayed to be?

Key Point Summary

- There is a very strong geographical pattern to voting in Britain, a clear North–South divide.

- The two main political parties secure far more seats than votes due to the voting system.

- By 2010 most people who voted in Britain did not get what they voted for.

6

INEQUALITY

… income, poverty and wealth

Underlying most of the maps and social relationships discussed in this book are the inequitable geographical distributions of income and poverty. These patterns are long established. Some of the inequalities shown over the next few pages are similar to patterns seen several hundred years ago. What is new is the wide extent of inequalities in poverty, wealth and income in Britain now. The size of the gap between those who have a great deal of money and those who have very little is without recent historical precedent, as are the sheer numbers of those living in poverty or on very high incomes. Such inequalities can become further entrenched as high incomes can be saved as wealth which in turn generates income. In Chapter 8 we consider some changes over time. Here we concentrate on the situation the British found themselves in at the start of this century.

Two sources of information are used in this chapter. The first source is two reports from Barclays Bank, published in 2002 and 2003 on the Internet, profiling parliamentary constituencies in England and Wales according to the then estimated incomes of Barclays' customers. These estimates were made from summing the steady streams of income entering customers' current accounts. Thus all forms of income were included and these figures relate to income most often after income tax had been paid. Estimates have been made here for incomes in Scotland by establishing the relationship between the Carstairs deprivation index and the log of income and projecting figures for Scotland from that. For Northern Ireland no income or similar deprivation index was available and so data is missing from the province. Compared to Britain, incomes are generally lower and poverty is higher in Northern Ireland.

The second source of information used here are the components of the United Nations Development Programme (UNDP) Human Poverty Index for Britain released by parliamentary constituency, again published on the Internet but a little earlier than the Barclays data, in 2000. These components include the functional illiteracy rate of adults, people's premature death rate (on which Chapter 7 concentrates), the then long-term unemployment rate and the proportion of people living on below half of average incomes. These could be readily aggregated to the European constituencies used in this book. The patterns they show are not dissimilar to how we think poverty is distributed amongst the population some ten years later, although right now we wait for the 2011 census to be sure of our facts. It is also useful to use these statistics from a decade ago as they remind us that even before the economic boom and crash there were huge disparities between the income and wealth of people in Britain; it was just that then people thought *a rising tide would lift all boats*.

The two sources of information used in this chapter show much the same picture, but each from different ends of the income scale. Together they illustrate how poverty does not exist without affluence, and affluence is not obvious without poverty. If there were very little poverty in Britain, the rich would be far less rich than they are. Without the rich there would similarly be far less poverty. For people to be rich others have to be poor, but not necessarily in the same places. Studying inequality requires studying both rich and poor simultaneously. While there is a great deal of information available on poverty, there is usually very little on affluence. Thus, to counter this, we begin with the highest income earners in the land.

In 2002 roughly 3% of Barclays' customers received an income of more than £60,000 a year, as estimated by the Bank. Comparisons with other sources of data suggest that this was a representative sample. Figure 6.1 shows how that proportion varied across the UK, from 8% in London Central to 1.2% in Glasgow and the Midlands (West). In most of the UK the proportion was less than 3%. In seven areas it was greater than 5%. However, an income of £60,000 may not sound very high to you, if you are from a wealthy family. It is, for most people, a fortune. In 2011 average incomes fell, before then incomes tended to rise faster than inflation and high incomes often still rise over time much more than inflation, than the cost of goods and services, does.

Figure 6.1 shows where the best-off people in Britain lived, and still live today, in terms of their incomes, which are mainly from earnings but can include pensions and any other regular sources (such as interest on savings). Although the map is not showing the distribution of wealth, which we turn to briefly at the end of this chapter, a great deal of these incomes will be turned into various forms of wealth. Income becomes wealth most obviously through paying high mortgages and securing housing wealth, but also from contributing to what will be high pensions in the future, or paying for children's education to ensure that they attend prestigious universities and become wealthy themselves. Look back over the maps in the preceding five chapters. To what extent were the patterns you were seeing there reflections of this geography of affluence?

In 2003 in each European constituency average income ranged from between £17,817 in Glasgow to £31,045 in London Central (Figure 6.2). The national average income of Barclays' customers was £21,851. Note that this average excludes people who do not have bank accounts, but also those too rich to have normal bank accounts. The overall effect is that this income is quite close to officially estimated average household incomes in Britain. Again the geographical inequalities are stark. The UK is cut in half roughly along the £21,000 mark.

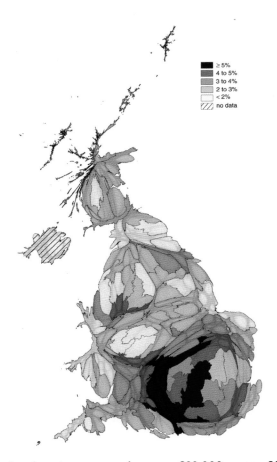

Figure 6.1 Barclays' customers earning over £60,000 a year, 2002

Source: Barclays Bank data aggregated to European constituency and estimated for Scotland. Availlable at www.newsroom.barclays.co.uk (accessed 14/8/2002).

Average salaries in the far south west, south and east London and in a handful of other areas in the South were (and remain) low, and just two areas of the North exceed this average. People were (and now even more are) paid more in the South of England. Part of the reason for this is London weighting on some salaries, but that is only a small part of the explanation. Barclays Private Clients (BPC), who produced the survey, suggested another reason, which we will consider next. Incidentally, BPC is the 'wealth management arm of Barclays, serving one million clients in the UK and around the world in the areas of financial planning, investment and banking. BPC has some 25% of the 'big ticket' mortgage market (£250,000 plus) in England and Wales. Their interest is in the rich.

Figure 6.3 shows data that Barclays released simultaneously to that shown in Figure 6.2 but now with average earnings roughly adjusted to reflect the regional cost of living. The comparable data for Scotland was estimated for this

Figure 6.2 Barclays' customers' average earnings per year, 2003

Source: Barclays Bank data aggregated to European constituency and estimated for Scotland. Available at www.newsroom.barclays.co.uk (accessed 14/8/2003).

book using the regional weighting they included for Roxburgh and Berwickshire constituency (which they published as if it were part of England). What this map suggests is that, once costs of living are taken into account, London contains two of the poorest income areas in Britain. The incomes of many people in the North and West of England are made to rise by their adjustment! In reality all incomes apart from those of a few rich landlords (and lenders to mortgagees) are reduced when housing costs are taken into account, but for now we'll not re-adjust Barclays' data.

Figure 6.3 suggests that back in 2003, after housing costs were adjusted for, most regions contained an area as affluent as London Central, and the Scots were particularly well off. The bulk of costs of living differences were housing costs. Although housing may be expensive for those who try to buy a house in the South when they are young, such costs are not wasted money. They are costs that are slowly being transferred to wealth. As house prices in London were still rising in 2011 while falling in much of the rest of Britain, viewed today this picture of income inequality is a little disingenuous. Nevertheless, this is how affluent the average young person may have felt in each area and thus also an indication of how rich a recent university graduate with a mortgage may have felt in the recent past, shortly after securing a good job. Remember again, though, that those in the South with mortgages were amassing considerable potential wealth while sometimes feeling temporarily poor.

Feeling poor and being poor are very different things. In Britain around the year 2000, roughly one in six people lived below the poverty line, as then defined by the UN, having an income less than half the median average. By 2009 over one in five had an income below 60% of the median, the EU definition. By 2011 The Joseph Rowntree Foundation was reporting that the numbers living

Figure 6.3 Barclays' customers' adjusted earnings per year, 2003

Source: Barclays Bank data aggregated to European constituency and estimated for Scotland. Available at www.newsroom.barclays.co.uk/ (accessed 14/8/2003).

in deep poverty, on just 40% of medium earning, had been rising for all of the last decade.

Figure 6.4 shows where people on poverty incomes lived in 2000. The map today will be very similar, although inequalities are now a little starker, poverty rates probably rising more where they were highest before. In no area were less than one-tenth of the population living in poverty; there are people trying to live on poverty incomes everywhere. However, rates of poverty measured in this way are generally twice as high in the North as in the South, and are clearly highest in Glasgow.

There is a very strong relationship between the maps in Figure 6.4 and Figure 6.1, with one exception. In no area where more than 4% of the population earn over £60,000 does income poverty exceed 20%. In all areas where those living in income poverty exceed 20% of the population, high earnings do not exceed 3%.

Figure 6.4 People living on below half average income in Britain, 2000

Source: A component of the UNDP Human Poverty Index, see Appendix in Seymour, J. (for UNED-UK) (2001) *Poverty in Plenty: A Human Development Report for the UK*, London: Earthscan Publications Ltd.

The one exception is London Central, with both the highest proportion of high earners and one-quarter of its population living below the income poverty line. In the centre of London the income-rich and income-poor live very close together. Elsewhere, more often than not, the income-rich pay, through their housing costs, not to live too near the income-poor.

There are many poor people living in London, and they are poor because their incomes are low. During 2011 attempts began to be made by the government to alter housing benefit rules in a way that was aimed to begin to force the poor out of the centre of the capital during 2012. However, those living legally on benefits could easily be replaced by others living a more precarious existence but drawn by the same opportunities and the very strong market for services that have been in London for so long: the rich.

Figure 6.5 shows the relationship between mean average earnings and the ratio of low to high earnings, combining data from the UNDP and Barclays. Average earnings can be predicted by the ratio of income-rich to income-poor people in an area in all areas except London Central. In Glasgow there were 25 people living on less than half national average income for every person living

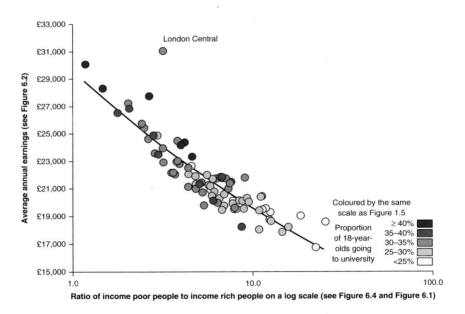

Figure 6.5   High, low and average earnings in Britain around 2001

Note: Coloured by the same scale as Figures 1.5, 1.7, 2.4, 2.9 and 5.7 to allow comparison with those maps and diagrams.

Source: Barclays Bank data aggregated to European constituency and estimated for Scotland. Available at www.newsroom.barclays.co.uk (accessed 14/8/2003); Seymour, J. (for UNED-UK) (2001) *Poverty in Plenty: A Human Development Report for the UK*, London: Earthscan Publications Ltd.

on £60,000 or more. At the other extreme, in Surrey, there are 1.2 people living on a poverty income for every one who is income-rich. Put another way, to be able to estimate the proportions of people who are very rich and very poor you need only know average incomes in each area. The only exception to this generalisation is London Central. The circles are coloured by young peoples' chances of getting to university as they appear more influenced by local levels of income and income inequality, as shown in this figure, than by GCSE results as shown earlier in Figure 5.7.

Incomes are particularly unevenly spread in London Central. Everywhere else the profile of inequality is similar. People are income-poor because in every area incomes are unevenly distributed in similar ways. In poorer areas there are more poor people; but there are poor people too in affluent areas. The one exception to this pattern, central London, is a peculiar place where incomes are even more unequally distributed than elsewhere as there are more very rich people than average central London incomes would suggest, but also more very poor people living there. Elsewhere the story is simpler.

There are high rates of income poverty in the North because there are low average incomes in the North. There are high rates of great affluence in suburban parts of London and the Home Counties because there are high average incomes there. Concentrations of poverty will, of course, reduce average incomes and concentrations of wealth raise them, but the relationships shown in Figure 6.5 do not simply imply that. Instead, they imply that income poverty is part of the spectrum of income inequality, as is affluence. Incomes tend to be higher for people who have more control over money. Bankers, for instance, can simply choose to pay themselves more from their banks.

The inequalities of modern life in Britain can lead to many people thinking there is no point in fighting back that much, that the poor will always be with us, in large numbers, and that the rich will always be so rich. Consider now Figure 6.6, which depicts levels of poverty in Britain, and see just how similar the map of poverty is to the map of abstaining in elections (Figure 5.5 in this book). There are many ways in which poverty can be measured. To be poor means to have both low income and low wealth. As access to information on wealth is limited, the UNDP index uses a series of internationally available proxy measures to estimate levels of poverty.

The rates in Figure 6.6 have been scaled to agree nationally with the Breadline Britain measure of poverty – a consensual measure which involves asking a large sample of people what they consider to be necessities for life in Britain. The measure counts as poor those households which do not have access to those necessities and then estimates their number. Around the year 2000, some 25% of households in Britain were poor by this measure, almost identical tothe proportion of households (rather than people) living at below half average income (Households Below Average Income – HBAI) after housing costs. Around 1991 the Breadline proportion was nearer 21%. For the 84 areas used here, the HBAI (Figure 6.4) and the UNDP index correlate with the Breadline index at

0.986 and 0.988 respectively. All maps of poverty are for practical purposes near identical no matter what measure is used.

Not only do different maps of poverty as estimated by slightly different measures tend to look identical to each other, but so many aspects of life are so closely connected to poverty that other maps can appear nearly identical to poverty maps.

Figure 6.6   Levels of poverty in the UK by UN definitions, 2000

Source: A component of the UNDP Human Poverty Index, see Appendix in Seymour, J. (for UNED-UK) (2001) *Poverty in Plenty: A Human Development Report for the UK*, London: Earthscan Publications Ltd., Northern Ireland data from Democratic Dialogue Report 16 (2003).

Figure 6.7 shows the proportion of adults aged 16–65 who are functionally illiterate. Being functionally illiterate means not being able to read and write at the most basic level expected of people in the UK (see Further Reading below for more details).

Almost all the areas of Britain where *less* than one-seventh of people of adult ages are functionally illiterate are in the South. The proportion is more than one-sixth in all of Scotland, in Northern Ireland and in 15 other areas in the North, but it is only at this level in the South in two areas of London. Compare this map of adults to that of children in Figure 3.1. Most of the places where two or more children do badly at age 11 for every child who does well are also the places where adults in the past more often did poorly out of their education.

Figure 6.7   Proportion of adults who are functionally illiterate in the UK, 2000

Source: A component of the UNDP Human Poverty Index, see Appendix in Seymour, J. (for UNED-UK) (2001) *Poverty in Plenty: A Human Development Report for the UK.* Northern Ireland data from Denny et al. (1999) Literacy and Education in Ireland, *The Economic and Social Review,* 30 (3): 215–226.

Over time levels of literacy should rise, but for those groups with the lowest levels to begin with, the recorded rises since 2000 have been minuscule; and people whose literacy and numeracy is said to be very good in Britain still often make simple mistakes. Poor education for the worst-off may breed complacency amongst the best-off. It is not hard to appear clever in countries where so many do so badly in education.

A few years ago there was an increase in children in the middle of the distribution doing better, and also of the best-off fifth of children amongst the poorest fifth of schools getting to university a little more often. In 2010 the proportion of 19-year-olds lacking what's called a basic 'Level 2' qualification fell to 21% as many young adults carrying on at school until that age were helped hugely, financially, by the introduction of educational maintenance allowances. But then the allowances were scrapped in late 2010 by the coalition government. Applications to universities fell in 2011. Fees rose. Currently there are few signs that educational inequalities will fall.

Simply being able to read and write at a functional level should be seen as normal and not as an accepted problem for a minority of the population. Only a few decades ago it was not necessary for many people to be functionally literate to be able to lead a good life. In a few decades' time, maps like this may be drawn of the information technology (IT) illiterate – and they may well look much the same.

Another component of the UN Poverty Index is premature mortality, measured here in Figure 6.8 as simply the proportion of people dying before their 60th birthday. By the end of the twentieth century over one-fifth of people in Glasgow did not live this long, and over one-eighth of people in almost all of the North died before reaching age 60. In the South such high mortality rates were only seen in four areas of London.

All the components of the Human Poverty Index are related to each other. Premature death is not only an indicator of poverty but also one of its main outcomes. Not all forms of death are hastened by poverty; a few are even the products of affluence, as Chapter 7 next illustrates, and there are many other factors which impact upon our health. However, growing up in poverty mostly shortens lives as well as increasing children's chances of never learning to read or write properly, diminishing adults' chances of getting a good job and of earning or receiving a decent income. If fewer of us understand numbers, and hence what they are doing, it is also easier for bankers to take more money out of our banks as their pay. If poverty is high, then one set of people also get to live to vote at fewer elections than their richer neighbours, so those who might oppose the rich each have a little less political power.

The last map here, Figure 6.8 shows where the people who do not feature on most of the maps and graphs described so far lived; that is, the people who could have expected to be living in these countries by the turn of the millennium, given when they were born, but who were not here then because they had died young. The majority of those deaths were very strongly related to the human landscape in which they were living. In the affluent European constituencies the majority that died young will have died within their poorer enclaves.

To illustrate just how close the relationship between these indicators can be, consider Figure 6.9, which shows how it is possible to predict the proportion of adults unable to read and write properly from the proportion of households in each area on below half average incomes (and both are closely related to university entry rates, used to colour the dots). Put roughly, in every area, for every 100 adults, eight will be functionally illiterate, with a further one who is illiterate for every two households living on below half average incomes. Of course this illiteracy is a product of poor education in the past, and so it could be claimed that it is the illiteracy, from that lack of education, which has led to low incomes. This will be partly true. But what led to the poor education of children in these areas in the past?

≥ 15%
14 to 15%
13 to 14%
12 to 13%
< 12%
no data

Figure 6.8 Proportion of the population dying by the age of 60 in Britain, 2000

Source: A component of the UNDP Human Poverty Index, see Appendix in Seymour, J. (for UNED-UK) (2001) *Poverty in Plenty: A Human Development Report for the UK,* London: Earthscan Publications Ltd.

Most areas that are poor now were poor half a century ago. A uniform standard of education was not provided across the UK then, as it is not now, and it will not occur in future unless we begin to behave differently. Children from poorer backgrounds and areas then were much less likely to pass the 11-plus as compared to their more affluent peers. There were more grammar schools per pupil in affluent areas and the map of people's relative chances of getting a university place was just as uneven, if not more so, although there were far fewer such places.

There is a circularity here whereby poverty in the past led to worse education, employment, health and housing, which in turn all increased people's chances of being poor in the future and then increased their children's chances of receiving relatively worse education, employment, health, housing and so on despite the general levels of these services improving. This process is amplified geographically most simply because the services are provided at an area level for groups of people, not for individuals, through school classrooms, firms' offices, the wider collective environment and the general building and maintenance of settlements.

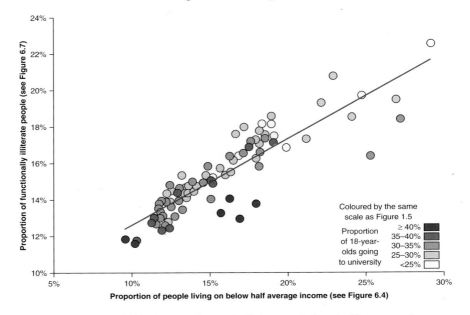

Figure 6.9 Rates of illiteracy and people living on below half average incomes

Note: Coloured by the same scale as Figures 1.5, 1.7, 2.4, 2.9, 5.7 and 6.5 to allow comparison with those maps and diagrams.

Source: Seymour, J. (for UNED-UK) (2001) *Poverty in Plenty: A Human Development Report for the UK*, London: Earthscan Publications Ltd. (data included in the appendix).

The direction of causality is perhaps a little less ambiguous when premature mortality is related to low incomes, as in Figure 6.10. In every area around the year 2000 roughly seven people out of every 100 died before age 60; you can add to that a further one premature death for every three households living on below half average income. However, again it could be argued that high rates of illness, preceding premature death, will result in fewer people working in poorer areas and thus in incomes being lower. Again though, you need to consider why more people were ill in these places in the first instance. To update this figure we need to wait for 2011 census results to tell us how many people are alive aged over 60 in each area. Again the circles are coloured by university entry rates, as in most of the recent scatterplots in this book, to show the general clustering and exceptions that occur.

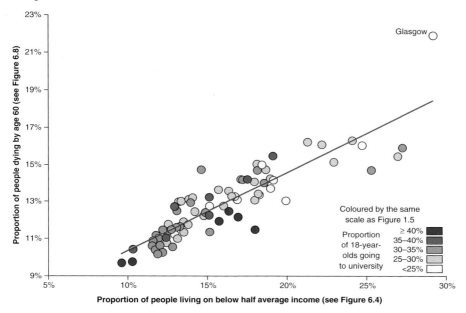

Figure 6.10 Rates of death and people living on below half average incomes

Note: Coloured by the same scale as Figures 1.5, 1.7, 2.4, 2.9, 5.7, 6.5 and 6.9 to allow comparison with those maps and diagrams.

Source: Seymour, J. (for UNED-UK) (2001) *Poverty in Plenty: A Human Development Report for the UK,* London: Earthscan Publications Ltd. (data included in the appendix); UK population Census 2001 and calculated for this book.

Poverty begets poverty and, it can be argued, is, in aggregate over time, largely a product of the greed of the affluent. It is the affluent who tend to have the power to share resources more fairly among all children in a country; they not only tend to end up going to university so often, and then fall into positions of responsibility much more frequently, tend to influence opinion as they write newspaper articles, create TV stories and draft school textbooks, but they mostly work together to avoid having to better share the wealth out.

It is the affluent majority who tolerate and maintain the organisation of society, the map of our human geography, which ensures that the children of poorer people are worse fed, educated, housed and employed. It should thus come as no surprise in the future that graphs, showing even stronger associations than Figure 6.10, might well be drawn. The precursors to premature death among the population are being lined up more carefully geographically and socially than they were in the past.

Why, if all this is so obvious, should the affluent behave like this? Well, for a start, it is in their short-term interest and their children's medium-term interests to behave like this. Second, as the following exercise illustrates, it is often not as obvious that growing inequality begets greater poverty as a result of how this information tends to be reported. Third, people are only human: altruism, rationality and decency are learned, not inbred.

AN EXERCISE

Read the article below then follow the instructions after it.

Adding Up to Much Less

Paul Foot, the *Guardian*, Wednesday, 26 November 2003

> On September 26 [2003], the leader of the House of Commons, Peter Hain, was on the BBC's 'Newsnight' proclaiming the progressive reforms of New Labour. High on the list, he claimed, was the closing of the gap between rich and poor. 'If you look at the figures,' he said, 'the bottom tenth of the population have seen their incomes increase by 15%, while the top tenth have seen their incomes reduced by 3%. That's redistribution.'
>
> This seemed so unlikely that I contacted the Office of National Statistics (ONS), now attached to the Cabinet Office. To my surprise, the figures it gave me confirmed what Hain said. The earnings of the poorest tenth, they revealed, had risen steadily since 1997, but, astonishingly, the earnings of the richest tenth, after growing even faster every year until 2001, suddenly and sharply went down in 2002.
>
> I went back, twice, to the ONS, requoted the figures they had given me, expressed my doubts, and asked for an explanation. Back came the reply that the figures had been 'double-checked' and were 'correct'.
>
> No doubt about it, then. Peter was right and my scepticism was wrong. But wait. Early this month, the ONS sent me a new set of earnings figures, updated to 2003. They flatly contradicted the figures given to me previously. They showed a steady annual increase in earnings for both the poorest and the richest tenths at about the same rate from 1997 to 2003.
>
> What was going on? I consulted Incomes Data Services, a specialist in such matters. Its explanation was rather shocking. 'The ONS,' it said, 'has made a mistake. It has given you the upper quartile (quarter) figure for 2002 when it should have given you the highest decile (tenth).' The real

figures for the richest decile showed a steady rise in earnings in every year from 1997 to 2003. So, under New Labour, the rich are getting richer and the gap between rich and poor is getting wider.

The ONS now admits its error, and has apologised to me. Where does that leave Peter Hain? His spokesman tells me that Hain's claim on Newsnight was based on a survey by the Institute of Fiscal Studies, whose press release concluded: 'Focusing on (tax and benefit) measures that directly affect household incomes and spending shows a progressive pattern, varying from a boost of more than 15% to the incomes of the poorest tenth of the population to a loss of nearly 3% for the richest tenth'. That says, vaguely and almost incomprehensibly, something rather different to what Hain claimed.

Much more specific and reliable are the latest figures from the Inland Revenue on the distribution of marketable wealth – which includes rent, dividends and other windfalls of capitalism. They show that the richest 1% of the population had 20% of the nation's wealth in 1996 and, thanks to Peter Hain and New Labour, 23% in 2001. This is a bigger, quicker leap in the booty of the mega-rich than anything achieved under any other postwar government, including Thatcher's. As for the poorest half of the population, they had 7% of the wealth in 1996. And after the first four caring years of New Labour, their share dropped – to 5%.

The newspaper article contains seven paragraphs, nine percentages, 13 dates and 538 words. Newspaper articles are often written 'from the top' so that the reader receives most information early on and need not read to the end. However, in this case, without reading to the end you cannot understand the beginning. Most readers do not read to the ends of most articles which they begin, especially ones which are complex, and this article is unusually complex, although its author has written about as clear an account of events as is possible. Five people are involved:

1 Paul Foot – journalist who specialised in exposing corruption in the UK.

2 Peter Hain – MP and at the time Labour leader of the House of Commons.

3 ONS spokesperson – nameless representative of the national statistics agency.

4 IDS specialist – nameless 'independent expert' from a private company.

5 Hain's spokesperson – nameless governing political party worker.

What do you believe motivated each of the actors in this story? To what extent are the various motivations a combination of overly suspicious minds, over-enthusiasm, incompetence, maliciousness, disingenuousness or other motives? For instance, does the rich becoming richer in terms of income necessarily mean that the gap between rich and poor is becoming wider? Does Paul Foot confuse income with wealth and with what significant implications, if any? With such questions in mind write a fictional letter to be published in the newspaper from the point of view of either Peter Hain, the ONS, the IDS or Hain's spokesperson, either objecting to the piece or supporting it. Write the letter in pairs and then, as a class, act as the Letters Editor of the newspaper and select those three or four that read best for publication (vote on it). Remember that letters to newspapers tend to be very short and to the point. Now each write a fictional reply from the point of view of Paul Foot to one of the letters and select the letter that you think is most convincing as a group by vote. Finally, if you find this interesting, find out what has happened to trends in income and wealth in the UK since this article was written. If you can find this out, perhaps using the same methods Paul Foot used, can you then write an article on it which is clear, well-written and could potentially be published?

Conclusion

The question of inequalities in income, wealth and poverty, their extent and whether they are rising or falling over time is among the stock-in-trade subjects of the *Guardian* newspaper, which published Paul Foot's article. Few other newspapers take such issues so seriously, and these are difficult issues to write about because many readers find arguments about changing unequal shares difficult to follow.

Given levels of functional illiteracy in the UK, many papers are written so that they can be read and understood by the average 12-year-old or even a younger child. Levels of functional innumeracy in the UK are far higher and so you will find only the simplest use of statistics in newspaper articles. Counts are always preferred over percentages. Anything more complex than a percentage is normally taboo. Often the detail of a particular topical incident, such as an MP's comments being allegedly misleading, is written about most verbosely while the key issue remains a footnote. For instance, regardless of what actually occurred during the first two terms of the millennial Labour government, the most important inequality is that given in the last sentence of Paul Foot's article – the sentence least likely of all to be read.

Half the population of the UK has recourse to only one-twentieth of the UK's wealth, implying that the other half holds 95% of everything that can be given a monetary value. For half the population to have recourse to 19 times (95/5) more than the other half is the remarkably inequitable result of how we distribute our resources, the products of our labours, and the chances in life we pass forward to our children. Yet this is an inequality we have become so accustomed to that we – journalists, statisticians and other commentators – take it almost for granted.

We are used to gross inequalities in wealth in society, but we are sufficiently embarrassed by them as to make it very difficult to obtain figures that can be mapped. A large part of the inequality is monies held in the form of housing wealth, but to map those alone would leave out the even more inequitably distributed forms of wealth. These include money itself (often called 'savings'), stocks, shares and other more illiquid forms of wealth which can and should be extended to future pension entitlements, insurance cover and future benefits from inequitable state support (for instance, the predictable financial value of attending the most prestigious couple of universities).

Paul Foot's figures do not include many of these other forms of wealth, but even by his own interpretation of the official statistics, we are only 5 percentage points away from a situation in which half the population has nothing, or negligible wealth. The last time a government held a Royal Commission to uncover the detailed distribution of wealth, in the 1970s, it concluded that half had practically nothing of value. But nothing was done to change that. In early 2010 these figures were updated in an appendix of a government commissioned report, *An Anatomy of Economic Inequality in the UK*. In May 2010 the governing party was changed and the report was largely ignored.

People and governments generally only become galvanised about inequalities during times of national crises, such as those following the First and Second World Wars. Similarly, at the start of the twentieth century a Liberal landslide victory helped pave the way for many reforms which reduced inequalities in that century's first few decades. The post-Second World War Labour landslide victory resulted in both a change in government and a change in underlying ideals, which meant that for many decades (in the middle of the last century) levels of inequality were held historically low and in some cases reduced.

The Labour government in power at the time the first edition of this book was written also won on a landslide; partly due to the rejection of a regime that had allowed inequalities to grow at their fastest ever rate. I wrote in that edition that 'Whether this current government enacts policies which actually lead to any reduction in inequality has yet to be seen, as the *Guardian* article makes clear. It clearly partly wishes to, otherwise the leader of the House of Commons would not be making such boasts, but beneath the claims facts are harder to find. Any failure to reduce inequalities will result in the human landscape of the UK becoming every more ragged.'

Alongside many others, I have recorded elsewhere how inequalities in education and employment chances were reduced slightly during the tenure of the 1997–2010 Labour government, but that inequalities in income, wealth and health were allowed to continue to rise. Since early 2010 education and employment chances have become polarised again. The peaks and valleys of life chances will rise and deepen, cliffs become higher and slopes appear where there were once flat plains on these maps.

Human landscapes change much more quickly than the physical landscape upon which our lives are played out, but they are similar in ways other than simply their appearance. Just as the physical landscape, at least at its surface, is largely made up of layer upon layer of sediment from past landscapes, so too underlying the landscape of the human geography of the UK are layer upon layer of the bodies from such past formations.

As the human landscape changes its surface shape, layers of sediment are laid down beneath that. This sediment can be described in many ways. It is made up of the industrial and social past of society, of millions more lives than those currently on the surface. The simplest way in which to depict the sediment of society is perhaps to take another metaphor from physical geography – and look at our history from the point of view of the dead and how their bodies came to be where they are, when they died. So now we turn from inequality to mortality.

Further Reading

In the year 2000 the BBC reported that at least seven million adults in the UK were functionally illiterate. At the time of the 2001 general election there were about 44 million electors in the UK and not all adults were registered to vote. Thus between one-sixth and one-seventh of adults were illiterate. This story was posted on 29 June 2000. In a great example of innumeracy amongst the elite, the BBC headlined its story 'One in five UK adults "illiterate"'. For details, read the story to be found at http://news.bbc.co.uk/1/hi/uk/811832.stm.

Ten years later a stricter test suggested that across the UK one-fifth of school leavers were either functionally illiterate *or* innumerate, so there was little evidence of great improvement over time for those doing worst at school. As income and wealth inequalities rose, and poverty rates remained very high, it was people in the bottom fifth of society who saw the least improvement in both their lives and their children's life chances. For literacy, 'Data showed a "gentle rise" in standards between 1997 and 2004, but then a further plateau.' You can find the article that reported this levelling in the *Telegraph* newspaper, which also suggested that as a result 'One in five teenagers is practically unemployable after leaving school lacking the English and maths skills needed for everyday life'. As within the text of the newspaper story it said 'or' not 'and' (between functionally illiterate and innumerate) it is worth considering innumeracy at the bottom of society and these mathematical errors made by both BBC and *Telegraph* journalists, errors made by people who tended to reflect and well illustrate levels of 'ability' and limits in that 'ability' at the apex of Britain's very hierarchical society. Decide for yourself whether the journalist could add up at www.telegraph.co.uk/education/educationnews/7691919/Fifth-of-school-leavers-illiterate-and-innumerate.html in the story entitled 'Fifth of school leavers "illiterate and innumerate"', the *Telegraph*, 7 May 2010.

Key Point Summary

- Measured in large areas the share of high earners varies seven-fold, between 8.2% and 1.2%.

- The proportion of households living in poverty is as high as 42%, and as low as 18%, between the same areas.

- Literacy, numeracy and mortality distributions all closely follow these same geographical patterns.

Postscript

Paul Foot died relatively young in the summer of 2004. A record of his work was published in *Private Eye* magazine in the autumn of that year and in numerous newspaper obituaries earlier. An annual award for pioneering journalism is now given in his name: http://en.wikipedia.org/wiki/Paul_Foot_Award.

7

HEALTH

... the sedimentation of society

When, and of what, will you die? It's eight in the morning, although my body thinks it's 1 pm. This book is now two years overdue to reach the publishers. I am sitting in a hotel room in Philadelphia in which the windows are sealed. The air conditioning is set to heat the room to 72 degrees Fahrenheit, which I have just realised is identical to the temperature of the tropical fish tank I have at home.

Tropical fish in captivity tend to experience quite a high mortality rate, but set the temperature right, give them the right amount of food and light, and they live longer. What tends to kill them is stress from swimming around in a confined overcrowded environment, diseases when new fish are introduced into their tanks, their own wastes when the filter system in the tanks doesn't work, and the actions of other fish. Their mortality rates reflect all these things. If there has been a power-cut at home and my partner notices it, then she can reset the circuit breaker and their water will continue to be filtered, heated and lit. If she does not, there will be a 'catastrophic event' and I will have to clean out the tank on my return. Tropical fish are not very different from people in the influence that their environment has on their health. They simply have a little less power to alter it, and their lives run out faster.

I have just lit the second cigarette of the day and am drinking the third cup of strong black coffee, wondering whether the hotel will charge me (or rather my university) for the coffee that appeared to be free in the room but is probably not. I am eyeing up the complimentary chocolate bar 'jam packed with even more peanuts', the main constituent of which is chocolate and wondering whether it would make a good substitute for breakfast. I do not have a particularly healthy lifestyle, especially for a middle-aged academic, and yet – if you believe the numbers – I am just as likely to reach three score years and ten (and perhaps a further five) as the average man of my age from my country is (if not much more if I continue to smoke).

What I am squandering through my lifestyle are the advantages I gain through my job. The things I am worrying about are whether the coffee is free, why the window won't open and how the fish are back home. I just phoned the family to say I arrived okay, and they are fine. I thought it might sound a bit callous if I asked about the fish! My university has paid for me to attend a conference although no one will know if I am here or not. There are 58 concurrent sessions about to start; I will not be missed. I am being paid to write what I want, where I want, when I want. Compared to the vast majority of people walking below my sealed window, I have it easy.

I can afford to go on holidays and get a great many holidays in contrast to most Americans on the sidewalk below. I don't worry about the bills, heating or cost of food. I have a great deal of control over my environment. Of course, I could be hit by a taxi walking out of the hotel this evening, I could suddenly feel a pain on the plane home and find out that my heart does not have long to carry on working, or I could have a very bad reaction to those peanuts. I could be diagnosed with cancer very early, in say a decade's time. But, odds on, I will die of a heart attack, in England, in relative comfort, in my early seventies ... That was 2004. Since writing those words I have given up smoking, as have so many other people like me. Despite the addiction it became easier not to continue given who I mix with, so now you can assume I'll make it to my 'late seventies'. And there's a fifty-fifty chance I'll live a little longer. Life and death are not distributed fairly.

This chapter tells a story of how, in our death (and that which leads to its precise timing and nature), we collectively lay down a record of our lives. Figure 7.1 shows the basic geographical distribution of mortality rates in Britain in the years leading up to the 2001 census. The rates shown are direct age–sex standardised rates. What they show is the number of people who would have died in each area, given the mortality rates of that area between 1996 and 2000 and if that area had had the same population demography as England and Wales had in the early 1980s (for which the rate is set to 1.0).

Figure 7.1 and the nine that follow are for all ages and both sexes. At the extreme, in Glasgow, people were 40% more likely to die in a given year than on average, 66% more likely than in the area with the lowest mortality rate which was, and at this geographical scale very possibly still is, Dorset & East Devon. To know where people are more likely to die it is just as important to know how many people are alive in each place as it is to know the count of how many die. We only know with some accuracy how many are alive when they are counted in the census, and estimates are then made for how many people the census may have missed or double-counted. When the 2011 census data is released during 2012 and 2013, we can update the maps in this chapter. This may be harder to do in future. The 2021 census is currently cancelled. It may be reinstated, or an alternative thought of, so that in ten years' time ten-year-old maps are not being shown *as not just the latest maps, but the last of these maps*. For now, let's not worry about the future; let's just try to understand these maps of the recent past.

Imagine that each of the areas in the figure was not a place, but a fish tank. Then the further north and west you travel, barring a few tanks in and near

London, the worse the fish generally do. In general, it is the environments in these areas, these tanks, which result in the patterns you see, especially the past environments. However, in aggregate, people differ from fish in one crucial way. They can move between their tanks. The majority of people who die in Dorset & East Devon did not begin their lives there. They moved to that area later in life and were able to afford to do so. Conversely, the majority of people who began life in Glasgow left that city long before they died elsewhere in the UK or abroad. The lifetime migration of people amplifies the environmental inequalities between places.

Figure 7.1   All-cause mortality ratios in Britain, 1996–2000

Note: Age–sex standardised mortality rate, deviation from England and Wales national average of 1.0.

Source: Mortality records and population estimates, calculated for this book.

Within the overall geography of the dead, mortality by specific causes provides clues as to what it is about particular environments which leads to earlier or later deaths. In Figure 7.2 (but often a little differently in the eight figures that

follow) areas are highlighted where more than 40% additional deaths are due
to a particular cause in an area, more than 20% more, over average, under average or less than 20% fewer deaths than average are so caused. Variations are
wider by cause than for all causes combined.

Figure 7.2 Tuberculosis mortality ratios in Britain, 1996–2000

Note: Age–sex standardised mortality rate, deviation from England and Wales national average
of 1.0.

Source: Mortality records and population estimates, calculated for this book.

The first cause of mortality shown in Figure 7.2 is an old disease: tuberculosis
(International Classification of Disease, 9th revision, categories, ICD9: 10–18,
119 and 137). It accounted for only 0.08% of all deaths in England and Wales
by this period, two-thirds of the proportion 20 years ago. By 2010, it accounted
for the same proportion (now classified as ICD10, 10th revision: A15–A19). It is
a disease that you are unlikely to contract if you are healthy, and is spread by
infection, which can largely be controlled to prevent mortality. However, despite
all this, a person is seven times more likely to die of tuberculosis in Glasgow as

compared to the affluent enclave of North Yorkshire. These are the two extreme areas within the extreme categories, with categories as shaded on the map.

In London and other urban areas in England rates remained above average as international migration brought in (and still brings in) a steady stream of cases which were contracted abroad. In the poorest parts of Britain the disease continues to exist without the need for new introductions due to the poor housing environment suffered by many people living there. This map is a tiny part of the jigsaw of death by a cause which contributes to the overall rates being what they are where they are.

Figure 7.3   HIV disease infections mortality ratios in Britain, 1996–2000

Note: Age–sex standardised mortality rate, deviation from England and Wales national average of 1.0.

Source: Mortality records and population estimates, calculated for this book.

Figure 7.3 shows the geographical distribution of what is still a quite new infectious disease: that associated with HIV (ICD9: 42–44, 279). When this map was drawn fewer people died of this than of tuberculosis, just 0.05% of all deaths, but almost seven times more than two decades ago when the disease was just beginning to be diagnosed. By 2010 the proportion had risen to 0.08% of all deaths (ICD10: B20–B24). Infectious diseases in total accounted for only 0.61% of all deaths by 2000, which has risen to just above 1.05% by 2010 as other causes have diminished in importance. They are of interest here because they illustrate just how important geographical location is to people's chances of contracting and dying of such diseases and because, when the next major infectious disease sweeps round the world, when it hits Britain it is within these places that it is likely to kill most people first.

For the rich western world, HIV turned out not to be the major pandemic once feared. Rates are highest in central London, Edinburgh, North East Scotland and East Sussex & Kent south (around Brighton). These were areas with high proportions of single people and a lot of migrants, and/or injecting drug users and relatively high proportions of gay men. In each area the specific immediate reason why rates of death from these diseases were unusually high or low is unique to that area. But it would be wrong to see these as the underlying reasons why rates are high in these areas. Before HIV diseases reached Britain none of these groups was at any risk of contracting these diseases here (although of course they could easily contract them abroad). When the next new infectious disease arrives, the one thing we can be fairly sure about is that it will have most affect in areas where people mix most.

In contrast to infectious diseases, Figure 7.4 shows the distribution of deaths from lung cancer (ICD9: 162), which, in the years leading up to the 2001 census, accounted for 5.4% of all deaths in England and Wales and 6.5% of all deaths in Scotland. This is a massive number compared to infectious diseases, one cause being responsible for almost ten times as many deaths as from *all infections*. It has also been rising in recent years to account for just under 7% of all deaths in England and Wales by 2010 (ICD10: C40–C41), but is largely confined to people aged over 65 now.

Lung cancer is a disease of which the major cause is smoking, and yet the map of it is a great amplification of the distribution of smoking. People's rates of smoking in the last century did not vary across the UK as much as this map suggests, and the rates varied even less in the past when most of the tobacco responsible was consumed. In addition to rates of smoking, the map reflects the differing environments smokers lived in, which made them more or less at risk of the damaging effects of cigarettes. It also reflects the distribution of people working in industries where their environment could expose them to pollution that might increase the risk of this cancer.

It is particularly important to realise that this map also greatly reflects the movements (or lack of movement) of people to where they are most likely to die. In the past, rates of smoking in London were high, but people left London when they were young and so the smokers of London have been spread thinly across the South of England. People were more likely to move from north to south if they did *not* smoke, or to stop smoking if they moved south because there were fewer other smokers around them. Smokers were much more likely to remain within Glasgow than non-smokers who left that city to live more frequently somewhere else, or, to put it another way, those who stayed in many areas of Glasgow were more likely to carry on smoking, perhaps partly influenced by what was then occurring in Glasgow.

Figure 7.4 Lung cancer mortality ratios in Britain, 1996–2000

Note: Age–sex standardised mortality rate, deviation from England and Wales national average of 1.0.

Source: Mortality records and population estimates, calculated for this book.

The sedimentary record of human life, as laid down in our deaths, is as much about our movements as it is about the places in which we have lived. Figure 7.5 shows the distribution of deaths from skin cancer (ICD9: 172), which accounted for 0.26% of deaths in England and Wales and 0.20% in Scotland by 2000 as mapped here. The geography of skin cancer is clear and additional hours of sunshine in Devon, Cornwall and along the south coast will have contributed to this pattern, as will the overcast skies of the North and West and the lack of many skin colours other than white in much of the countryside. However, skin cancer can kill at older ages and thus by the time people have moved home and possibly region or even country several times. Furthermore, it is likely to have been partly exposure to sunlight in much warmer climes than Britain which contributed to many individuals contracting this disease, particularly former sailors, but also keen sunbathers.

Some of the pattern seen in Figure 7.5 is of the people who come to live along the south coast of England who are both more likely to have been exposed most to sunlight and not to have died of another disease before that exposure could result in cancer. Younger people are more likely to die of the most fatal form of melanoma. Skin cancers, on aggregate, are diseases of the more affluent in Britain and so their geography partly reflects people's residential choices and their choices

≥ 1.2
1.1 to 1.2
1 to 1.1
0.9 to 1
< 0.9
no data

Figure 7.5 Skin cancer mortality ratios in Britain, 1996–2000

Note: Age–sex standardised mortality rate, deviation from England and Wales national average of 1.0.

Source: Mortality records and population estimates, calculated for this book.

(made possible by wealth) in earlier years to be among the first generation to travel in large numbers abroad for their holidays. Maybe this is a large part of the reason why we see this particular pattern to these deaths. In just ten years these death rates have increased to approach 0.5% in England and Wales (ICD10: C43). This may well reflect skin-burn on holidays taken in the 1970s and 1980s having effects decades later. In the 1960s most people in Britain had no summer holiday.

Figure 7.6   Cervical cancer mortality ratios in Britain, 1996–2000

Note: Age–sex standardised mortality rate, deviation from England and Wales national average of 1.0.

Source: Mortality records and population estimates, calculated for this book.

The third cancer we consider here accounts for 0.21% of all deaths, less than one-hundredth of the 25% of all deaths which by 2000 was attributable to cancers (just over 30% by 2010). Cervical cancer (ICD9: 180, ICD10: C35) only kills women and has reduced in impact to almost 70% of its rate in the early 1980s, partly due to earlier screening and better treatment programmes. As a proportion of all deaths it now appears stable. Figure 7.6 shows some very clear patterns to this disease. The low rates around the Home Counties ring are very distinct, as are the high rates in Yorkshire and in the North West.

Unlike skin cancer, cervical cancer is a cause of death which contributes to the overall geographical pattern of mortality rather than one which helps to reduce geographical variations. Again, patterns of migration are key issues to understanding the map seen here. People partly live in the Home Counties as a result of migrating into them over the course of either their or their parents' lives. People at lower risk of contracting cervical cancer or with a higher chance of being successfully diagnosed with that cancer early and being treated are more likely to live in such places. There are many factors which lead to some groups of women being more likely to have this disease than others, but just as those factors are important, so too are the factors that lead women with those risks to come to be living in particular places in Britain.

Figure 7.7   Heart attack mortality ratios in Britain, 1996–2000

Note: Age–sex standardised mortality rate, deviation from England and Wales national average of 1.0.

Source: Mortality records and population estimates, calculated for this book.

While cancers account for one-quarter of all deaths, a degenerative disease of the circulatory system accounted for the largest proportion. Up to the year 2001 this was 40% (down to around 30% by 2010). Of these the largest numbers are attributed to simple heart attacks (ICD9: 410), responsible for 10.81% of all deaths in England and Wales and 14.56% of all deaths in Scotland by the start of this century. These proportions have been falling over time, but it will be many years before diseases of the heart are no longer the primary cause of mortality in Britain. The falls to 2010 have been dramatic, but partly due to more of these deaths being attributed to other forms of heart disease, so a straightforward comparison over time is difficult to make.

Many factors make some people's circulatory systems more susceptible to diseases than others. Smoking and diet are important, yet Figure 7.7 shows patterns which yet again cannot simply be accounted for by such variations in behaviour. These are the major diseases which contribute to the overall geography of mortality in the UK. Mortality rates in Scotland and parts of the North are simply too high to be purely a reflection of behaviour and social conditions there; rates in the south of London, through Hampshire to the coast, are too low for local (lower smoking) environments to simply be the cause of these patterns.

With the distribution of heart attacks, as with so many other measures of misfortune in Britain, yet again we are seeing a distribution which is partly the result of lifetime migration. People who have been healthier during their child-hood and working lives are more likely to have left the places with the highest rates. Such difference can be further amplified, as in places where rates are lower, the health service has tended to be less stretched and better able to treat early symptoms of disease.

Healthier people in poorer areas have tended to move out of those areas. At the same time healthier people in richer parts of the UK have tended to be among those most likely to move into the most affluent areas of those already more affluent regions. Thus, just as for heart attacks, we see very clear patterns from deaths attributable to strokes (cerebrovascular diseases; ICD9: 430–438), this collection of conditions being responsible around 2001 for 10.28% of all deaths in England and Wales and 11.98% of all deaths in Scotland (below 8% by 2010 as ICD10: 160–169).

Figure 7.8 shows how London's rates remain low, as London attracts ever more disproportionately the fit and those who are able to migrate there. However, Scotland, suffering from depopulation of its more moveable people in many areas, was left by the late 1990s with a population at far greater risk than average of dying from these causes. Of course, lifestyles in Scotland and London will differ, although more so now than they have in the past, and again rates of smoking are important. But if you look closely at the figures, you will see that relentlessly as you move from north and west to south and east, the rates of death from this disease fall.

Environments matter, but they are made partly by the movements of people, and cause people to move in particular directions. The deaths in these five years from strokes are laying down a very clear picture of many aspects to the lives of the past peoples of Britain, including how they came to live and die where they did. As strokes become less common as a cause of death, it has been in Scotland that the most benefit has been realised in very recent years, but other causes also rise in importance, and they tend to also rise more in Scotland than elsewhere.

Figure 7.8 Cerebrovascular disease mortality ratios in Britain, 1996–2000

Note: Age–sex standardised mortality rate, deviation from England and Wales national average of 1.0.

Source: Mortality records and population estimates, calculated for this book.

Causes of death not related to disease are labelled as 'external' under the classification of mortality. This is a misnomer in that almost all the actual underlying causes of deaths are external to the body of the person who has died. Only 3.2% of all deaths are due to such causes, the majority of which are due to

suicide, falls and motor vehicle accidents. Figure 7.9 shows the distribution of
one cause outside this group – fire (ICD9: 890–899, ICD10: X00–X09) – which
accounted for (and still accounts for) 0.07% of all deaths in England and Wales,
0.10% in Scotland.

Figure 7.9   Mortality caused by fire ratios in Britain, 1996–2000

Note: Age–sex standardised mortality rate, deviation from England and Wales national average
of 1.0.

Source: Mortality records and population estimates, calculated for this book.

What is most interesting about deaths from fires in Britain in the context of this
book is how they also reflect the overall pattern of mortality which is most clearly
related to the distribution of poverty, and the patterns of migration which result
from that distribution. But there are always caveats to such generalisations. Most
deaths from fire are due to smoke inhalation by people who are unable to escape
a fire or who are unaware of it. Figure 7.9 largely reflects the distribution of poverty, where people are more likely to live in homes without smoke alarms, with
dangerous wiring and, yet again, where more people smoke.

The most immediately dangerous fumes of a cigarette are from the fire it can light (thus they can kill in seconds as well as years). However, in addition to smoking, the map is also strongly influenced by where people live in flats. Even in affluent parts of London, rates are high where the population is crowded. Within those affluent parts, though, the rates tend to be highest where the population is most crowded of all. Overcrowding within the capital rises, as more and more of the people with the least money squeeze into the smallest of flats. It is the poorest that are at greatest risk in the places where mortality rates from this cause are highest.

Figure 7.10 shows the last of nine selected causes of death chosen here to illustrate how each either adds to or detracts from the overall pattern of death

Figure 7.10   Mortality ratios of suicide by hanging in Britain, 1996–2000

Note: Age–sex standardised mortality rate, deviation from England and Wales national average of 1.0.

Source: Mortality records and population estimates, calculated for this book.

in Britain and how many factors influence each individual distribution. Almost 1% of all deaths around the year 2000 were due to suicide or were 'undetermined accidents' (which are most likely to be suicide). That proportion is now rising, and by 2010 suicides and undetermined accidents accounted for 1.9% of deaths of all men, and 0.8% for all women (ICD10: X60–X84, Y10–Y34).

There are many ways in which people can kill themselves, but the most common method, particularly among men, is by hanging, which accounts for one-third of all suicides. When the map is considered, again we see the Home Counties ring: people who live here are less likely to kill themselves, especially in this way. It is in the periphery of Britain where rates are high, at the edges of Wales, in the North West and in urban and remote Scotland. Suicide is perhaps the simplest example to give of a cause of death influenced by people's environment.

There are very many reasons why people may seek to harm themselves, and why a proportion of those may manage to kill themselves, but in aggregate they reveal the geography that shows where some are more than twice as likely as others to resort to a ligature to hasten their own deaths. Thus, even how people choose to kill themselves has a geographical story. In the major cities, poisons and drugs are more common methods. In affluent areas, the fewer numbers who do resort to suicide are more likely to use the exhaust fumes from their cars. They are more likely to have both a car, and a garage.

AN EXERCISE

Table 7.1 lists the major causes of mortality in England and Wales in the year 2010, their ICD codes, disease label and the cumulative chance of dying of each cause of death (in the first column as measured out of 1024). Thus a man or boy has about a 5.8% chance of dying of a disease not listed in the table and a woman or a girl an 8.3% chance (see the first two numbers in the first column of the table below for where those percentages come from).

We can use the first column, the 'cumulative chance out of 1024', and a coin, to give each member of the class a cause of death at random, assuming that the patterns in the future are similar to those in 2010. The distribution of causes of death in the class should then reflect those in society as a whole.

To play the game each student needs a coin. Heads are '1' and tails are '0'. They will need to toss their coin 10 times to determine their allotted cause of death. This method is similar to that used in the exercise at the end of Chapter 6. Begin with a chance of 1 out of 1024. Toss the coin for the first time, if you get heads add 1, otherwise add nothing. Do this again a second time, but add 2 if you get heads, again nothing if you get tails. Do it again, adding 4 for heads; again, adding 8 for heads; again, adding 16; again, adding 32; again, adding 64; again, adding 128; again, adding 256; and again, adding 512 if you get heads. Ten heads and your number is 1024 and you are dying of an external cause (other). There are different chances for men and women (use the rows marked M and F below).

Table 7.1 Death rates per million population in England and Wales: selected underlying cause, sex and age-group, 2010

Cumulative chance out of 1024	ICD-10 code	Underlying cause		All ages	Death rates per million population										
					Under 1	1–4	5–14	15–24	25–34	35–44	45–54	55–64	65–74	75–84	85 and over
	A00–R99	All causes, all ages	M	6406	4637	194	106	454	760	1530	3222	8277	20509	56638	152699
			F	4581	4032	172	93	208	379	917	2140	5291	13093	40813	136937
58	U509, V01–Y89	Not listed below	M	365	4290	72	20	45	67	127	196	320	664	1998	9010
83			F	371	3670	60	24	35	55	84	127	239	553	2102	13921
79	C15	Malignant neoplasm of oesophagus	M	128	0	0	0	0	2	15	88	274	578	990	1352
93			F	44	0	0	0	0	1	4	24	71	187	429	699
98	C18	Malignant neoplasm of colon	M	119	0	0	0	1	4	12	57	188	518	1152	1945
112			F	84	0	0	0	0	4	13	46	120	336	845	1527
172	C33–C34	Malignant neoplasm of trachea, bronchus and lung	M	465	0	0	0	1	2	36	189	895	2330	4195	5121
178			F	299	0	0	0	0	3	24	165	669	1487	2480	2491
172	C50	Malignant neoplasm of breast	M	2	0	0	0	0	0	0	1	3	6	10	50
233			F	245	0	0	0	0	15	124	294	548	807	1442	2626
269	C51–C58	Malignant neoplasms of female genital organs	F	161	0	0	0	3	22	50	137	356	696	1046	1339
211	C61	Malignant neoplasm of prostate	M	238	0	0	0	0	0	2	17	177	822	2936	7624

(Continued)

Table 7.1 (Continued)

Death rates per million population

Cumulative chance out of 1024	ICD-10 code	Underlying cause		All ages	Under 1	1-4	5-14	15-24	25-34	35-44	45-54	55-64	65-74	75-84	85 and over
236	C81–C96	Malignant neoplasms of lymphoid, haematopoietic and related tissue	M	161	5	7	6	12	23	29	76	253	692	1459	2199
292			F	102	11	6	5	10	10	22	49	150	430	969	1444
383	C00–D48 (other)	II Other neoplasms (cancers)	M	916	19	19	20	26	58	166	527	1651	3848	7788	13154
413			F	542	17	23	19	22	44	116	337	974	2138	4595	8077
408	F00–F99	V Mental and behavioural disorders (mostly dementia)	M	160	3	0	0	13	56	76	60	64	189	1384	7241
454			F	184	0	0	2	4	11	25	19	43	165	1724	11430
444	G00–G99	VI Diseases of the nervous system	M	225	81	21	15	33	32	58	101	224	610	2418	5377
494			F	180	114	29	13	21	20	39	85	196	464	1743	5030
509	I21–I22	Acute myocardial infarction	M	406	0	0	0	2	11	61	254	620	1432	3731	8562
535			F	182	0	0	0	0	4	16	53	158	562	2081	5858
552	I26–I52	Other heart diseases	M	268	24	14	4	14	32	68	118	260	655	2375	9301
584			F	220	37	5	5	8	16	34	57	136	422	2095	10188
619	I60–I69	Cerebrovascular diseases	M	422	16	2	2	5	13	48	119	302	1094	4510	15984
673			F	396	20	1	1	4	9	28	97	207	801	4237	18400
636	I71	Aortic aneurysm and dissection	M	105	0	0	0	1	3	13	22	93	406	1286	2469
683			F	46	0	0	0	0	3	3	6	26	149	628	1400
767	I00–I99 (other)	IX (other) Diseases of the circulatory system	M	817	6	0	1	3	20	119	403	1169	2784	7670	20075
778			F	425	0	0	0	2	10	43	129	348	1145	4461	15959
808	J12–J18	Pneumonia	M	260	30	9	2	5	9	27	56	166	499	2298	12888
826			F	212	26	8	1	2	5	20	40	110	330	1869	11735

Death rates per million population

Cumulative chance out of 1024	ICD-10 code	Underlying cause		All ages	Under 1	1-4	5-14	15-24	25-34	35-44	45-54	55-64	65-74	75-84	85 and over
859	J40–J44	Bronchitis, emphysema and other chronic obstructive pulmonary disease	M	314	0	0	1	0	0	7	45	329	1217	3652	8294
873			F	212	3	0	0	0	1	5	40	264	903	2573	4231
894	J00–J99 (other)	X (other) Diseases of the respiratory system	M	219	40	12	5	6	10	27	55	177	611	2289	7600
907			F	152	51	11	9	6	11	21	43	103	377	1432	6130
919	K70–K77	Diseases of the liver	M	159	5	0	0	2	33	158	323	429	385	305	278
926			F	84	0	0	0	1	27	83	160	209	210	209	182
950	K00–K93 (other)	XI (other) Diseases of the digestive system	M	195	27	4	3	5	11	41	87	248	569	1892	5355
966			F	179	23	3	1	5	7	19	60	154	505	2001	5904
969	N00–N99	XIV Diseases of the genitourinary system	M	118	13	1	1	2	2	8	20	62	220	1290	5573
990			F	110	9	2	0	1	2	9	20	53	199	1157	5453
1001	V01–X59	Accidents (mostly car crashes)	M	198	40	24	19	160	194	198	191	177	246	815	2938
1013			F	101	28	19	9	43	51	63	76	89	158	607	2791
1020	X60–X84, Y10–Y34	Intentional self-harm; and event of undetermined intent	M	120	8	0	2	86	148	206	193	166	101	136	177
1021			F	37	0	1	1	30	38	57	64	54	42	42	42
1024	U509, V01–Y89 (other)	XX External causes of morbidity and mortality	M	26	30	9	5	32	30	28	24	30	33	59	132
1024		(other)	F	13	23	4	3	11	10	15	12	14	27	46	80

Source: ONS: Mortality Statistics: Deaths registered in England and Wales (Series DR), 2010. Available at www.ons.gov.uk/ons/publications/re-reference-tables.html?edition=tcm%3A77-230730.

This game may appear a little complex, but all it involves is in effect turning up to 10 tosses of a coin into a number between 1 and 1,024 to give a probability which can then be used to allocate a cause of death from Table 7.1. By reading down the first column until you come to your number or a number larger than it, it quickly becomes apparent which cause of death you have been allocated.

Here's a worked example. I start with the number 1 and toss tails, heads, tails, heads, tails, heads, tails, heads, tails, heads. My score is $1+0+2+0+8+0+32+0+128+0+512 = 683$. I decide I am male and look down the first column until I get to 767, the first number equal or greater than mine. I read across and see I am to die of 'IX (other) Diseases of the circulatory system'. Reading from further up the column in the table to see what I have just skipped I work out that this will be a more obscure disease of my heart and blood vessels, but not acute myocardial infarction (heart attack), Other heart diseases, Cerebrovascular diseases, or an Aortic aneurysm. Well, that doesn't sound too bad.

Having allocated each member of the class a cause of death at random, next work out which groups of causes are most numerous in your population – infectious diseases, cancers, diseases of the blood and so on. For the most common causes, see if you have people allocated similar causes within those groups. It is important to remember that these causes have been allocated at random. They mean nothing for the people specifically allocated a cause. Some congenital causes (which are mostly included in the first group) only kill young babies, for instance, and several causes largely only apply to either men or women. However, for the group as a whole the distribution should be interesting. Here are a series of questions you can ask:

1   Are there causes that people are concerned about, for instance accidents or pneumonia, which no one in your class has been allocated? Is this because they are rare or because of chance? If you think it is chance, try another random allocation of the class. If you are very good at maths, work out how many allocations you would have to make, given the size of your class, on average, until these causes were allocated.

2   What will kill the bulk of students in your class if they are representative of the population of England and Wales, and if future causes of death are distributed as they are now?

3   Can you think of any reasons why your actual causes of death may be different from those allocated by this procedure, even if future causes of death are distributed as they are now?

4   Which of the causes that have been allocated do you think students will be less likely to die of in the future and which more likely, and why?

5   Given the maps above and the location in which you are playing this game (if that is in Britain), how might your local geography influence these chances?

6   Finally, the table also includes information about the rates of death per million at particular ages. Ignoring the first general category of 'not listed below', what does kill most people of your group's average age?

Conclusion

In aggregate, people leave more messages from their deaths than each individual mortality does alone. The deaths of the people of Britain lay down the sediment of its human geography, sediment which reflects almost everything about their pasts. In the future, if disasters and wars do not have a great impact, the population may live longer than it has ever done. However, the spatial patterns of people's deaths could be even more distinct than those shown in the whistle-stop tour of mortality presented in the last few pages.

The determinants of premature mortality and longevity are becoming more spatially distinct. From people's environmental conditions in childhood and around the time of their birth, through to their behaviours as adults, the kinds of jobs they do and the rewards, freedoms, pressures and threats which they face, through to their recreational and retirement opportunities, the maps of these countries are changing and those changes will be reflected in the patterns of future deaths. Most importantly, migration patterning is becoming ever more distinct. People are sorting themselves out in space, by place, more and more keenly as every year passes, as house prices diverge, and as yet greater proportions of the population leave home to attend university (at least they did until the year 2011).

Above all else, two forces, poverty and migration, create and amplify the spatial patterns revealed in our mortality. They also strongly influence our collective behaviours which are the immediate precursors of some of the biological causes of our physical deterioration. Although we have no very accurate figures on the geography of smoking, those estimates that have been made suggest that the map strongly mirrors that of poverty. Of course, there are exceptions, but they are becoming less and less evident and, as social groups are becoming ever more corralled together through their differential migration, they increasingly conform to what is normal for that place and that group.

When I first wrote these words it was at this precise point that I took a break from writing. I went downstairs and had my late breakfast and then I stepped out of the hotel for a smoke. There were over 5000 delegates at the conference which I was skipping to get my writing done. Only one other person from inside the building was smoking on the pavement with me. Outside, many of the people going about their normal business had cigarettes in their hands: the bus-boys on their breaks, the secretaries on an errand, the taxi drivers standing by their cars waiting for the next fare. Twenty-first-century America can partly be seen as a model for what twenty-first-century Britain could soon be.

The middle-aged, middle-class academics are going to live for a long time. Their hearts will be stronger, they will be less susceptible to certain cancers and they will be among the first to benefit from new cures for others. They will die later of causes most associated with very old age. I could have also added that they would be most likely to have given up smoking very soon. In contrast, the people who clean their hotel rooms, serve their drinks, drive them in taxis to meetings, look after their children, mend their houses and care for them in their old age are unlikely to benefit more than a fraction from the increased longevity that comes from greater overall affluence. This will be blamed on the poor themselves, on their poor life-styles, on their behaviour, on their claimed lack of aspiration, on their supposed weaknesses. But if it were not for them, what would the affluent have and how would they benefit from their affluence to the advantage of their health?

Without the poor, the rich would have to clean their own rooms, make their own food and drive themselves around. They could not rely on others to arrange their holidays, staff their resorts, clean their offices and take their orders. They would have to look after their children when they were very young all day every day and their parents when they were old. The rich could not have jobs where they were paid to travel round the world and could type books about the plight of the poor while other people looked after their basic needs. Most impor-tantly, internationally, the rich countries of the world would not be rich were it not for the efforts of peoples in the poorer nations of the world. We simply could not all consume what the rich consume and we (rich) need the poor to make what we consume. The health of the affluent is as much a product of poverty as is the premature mortality of the poor – worldwide and at home.

Four thousand words, four cigarettes, six cups of coffee, one breakfast and a quick break later and I was finished. In theory, and on average, what I had smoked that morning should have reduced my life expectancy by three quarters of an hour. The coffee and the cooked American breakfast didn't do much good either. Apart from the quick walk through the lobby I had hardly any exercise. This hotel appeared to have elevators and no stairs. I had been breathing air recycled through a conditioning system. The temperature remained exactly 72 degrees Fahrenheit. Yet I had been doing exactly what I had chosen to do. I had not had to take any instructions from anyone else. I took no phone calls, received no emails, no students had been able to interrupt my work – I was 4000 miles away from them. I found it hard to imagine a degree of freedom much greater than this when I first wrote these words. Since then I have become freer. I have realised just how lucky I am, and I try to use that luck for some purpose.

When civil servants in London were monitored to assess the determinants of their health many years ago it was found that those with jobs like mine, which they often described as 'stressful', but which in reality were not, tended to live longer than civil servants on lower-pay grades even when those with more free-doms had what appeared to be worse lifestyles in terms of their health-related behaviour. Had I spent the few hours it took to write this chapter, and then revise it five year later, doing something directly for somebody else, and if that was what I normally did every day, then according to that evidence, the slow cumulative effects of being subservient to others would have done more damage to me than what currently appears to be a very unhealthy few hours spent typing these words. That is all, of course, on aggregate. For any individual, anything can happen, and averages are less useful than advice to look after their bodies and their minds. But, if you are free to think, not just free to try to make money, but really free, what more is there? What about others' misery?

Further Reading

There is huge controversy concerning what are the factors which have improved the health of people living in Britain so much in recent years. Very large numbers gave up smoking in the last six decades and the extent to which they did so is largely reflected in differing improvements in mortality and the changing main causes of deaths in the population some two or three decades later. However, work on studying civil servants found that those higher up the hierarchy who smoked could live longer, on average, than those lower down who did not. That work was carried out by Michael Marmot and a large research team at University College London. To see what that team is doing now have a look at its website www.instituteofhealthequity.org.

Michael Marmot also conducted the 'Fair Society, Healthy Lives' review for government in Britain in 2010. It was a very thorough piece of work, but it had its critics, including this author and a friend. Here is what we said: www.danny dorling.org/?page_id=1917; the formal reference for that paper was: Pickett, K. and Dorling, D. (2010) Against the Organization of Misery? The Marmot Review of Health Inequalities, *Social Science and Medicine*, 71, 1231–1233. It was just three pages long appearing after 1230 other pages of papers in volume 71 of the *Journal of Social Science and Medicine*. You could easily miss it, so have a look on the Web. I promise not to refer to anything else I have written if you do!

Key Point Summary

- Everybody dies, but some die too early, and there are a wide variety of rare causes of death.

- There are distinct geographical patterns to be seen in premature mortality by cause of death.

- It is far easier to live a healthy life if you are free, especially free of others' orders.

8

WORK

... the segmentation of society

Matters such as whether people work, the work that they do, how well they are rewarded for it and almost every other aspect of their employment are greatly influenced by geographical location in the UK. Furthermore, the way those conditions of employment are changing, what work is available, in which industries and the changing extent to which the population is able to carry out this work are also strongly geographically patterned. To understand both how these patterns are changing and what they are changing into requires simultaneously observing processes of both dispertion and concentration. The maps in this chapter are attempts to show both of these distributions together for ten selected aspects of the labour market.

People in the UK are segmented, that is, partitioned into groups, largely on the basis of the work which they do or have done, which jobs their parents do or have done, and the financial rewards they have received for such work. This segmentation is as much spatial as social and, over time, has become more geographically distinct. There have always been geographical divisions in the labour market, but in the recent past people doing a wide variety of jobs tended to live closer together. Before cars became as ubiquitous as they are today, before many of the new motorways were built, before people had the kind of fear of living with others that they have now, there was more geographical mixing of the population, and labour market segmentation tended to occur within places and between social classes.

Today segmentation by income levels is increasingly found as much between places as within places. Within smaller neighbourhoods there is less differentiation between social classes. The extent to which this generalisation holds varies across the UK and depends on how you define a place. London is an exception, for instance, in that in many ways it is an increasingly heterogeneous place. However, if you partition London, as is done in these maps, then that heterogeneity is largely confined to the very centre of the capital.

Labour markets express the demand for people in places. In some areas the demand remains very high; many people move into an area; they tend to be well rewarded and those who cannot contribute the skills which are required become slowly priced out of the area. In other areas there is very little demand for people and that demand is dropping. In these places demand was often higher in the past and so there is a surplus of human beings as far as the market for their labour is concerned. People tend to leave these places; the more able leave the fastest. Increasing numbers of people are permanently sick or disabled in such areas, unable to work mostly through the effect that being redundant to the market has had on their health, partly perhaps because this is a rational reaction to the vagaries of markets.

Although unemployment, as officially recorded, fell everywhere in the ten years that the maps in this chapter can concentrate on (1991–2001), there was simultaneously no significant rise in employment and jobs became less secure and, in many cases, more demanding and/or menial than they once were. This may have been a major cause in the overall rises in illness rates which are reported at the end of this chapter, rises which were distinctly geographical in character – as are all aspects of labouring in the UK.

It is only the population census that can reveal if there has been no real rise in employment. The same person can work at two or even three different jobs, one in the evening and one at weekends, say. So employment surveys may show rising numbers of jobs, but these may not represent more people being paid, just a few people having to work a huge number of hours that no one else is regulating. Similarly, the rise in jobs that occurred between 1991 and 2001 consisted mostly of university students working part-time and only the census records that these were also people trying to study. We need the 2011 census to tell us how work has changed for people over the course of the last decade.

The historical legacy of industry in the UK is etched into our landscape and explains much of our current human geography. Places typified by industries in continuous decline tend to show a relative decline in most other aspects of the lives of the people who live there. Figure 8.1 shows both the proportion of all people working in manufacturing in each area in 1991, and how that proportion changed by 2001.

In all these figures that follow, areas are shaded according to both whether proportions of people above or below national average were in an employment category and as to whether these proportions have risen or fallen during the previous ten years. Figure 8.1 shows that, by 2001, almost all of the UK was typified by either relatively high rates of employment in manufacturing, which have fallen, or low rates, which have also fallen over time. What the map cannot show is that in the South these rates had fallen because other industries had replaced manufacturing employment, whereas that is not the case in the North. The maps that follow later in this chapter are needed to see that.

The greatest fall, of the loss of one-third of the jobs in manufacturing industry in one area, occurred in Birmingham East over the course of the 1990s. That fall is known to have accelerated since then, but as yet we cannot be sure how bad it became because, among much else, we do not know how many people left that area to go to live in another country since 2001. What we do know now, in hindsight, is that the falls shown here were on-going and not the end of a readjustment to less manufacturing in Britain.

Legend:
- High, rising
- High, falling
- Low, rising
- Low, falling

Figure 8.1 Employment in manufacturing in the UK, 1991–2000

Source: UK population Censuses 1991 and 2001, calculated for this book.

In stark contrast to manufacturing, employment in the banking and finance industries rose throughout the UK during the 1990s, as Figure 8.2 documents. The largest rise was in central London where an additional 8% of the population became employed in this industry in the 1990s, bringing the total in this sector up from 11% to 19% of the entire population, as compared with 8% nationally.

By 2001 more people worked in this sector nationally than in all of the manufacturing industries combined (which by then employed 7% of the population of the UK, a share that was falling). Work in the finance sector became most concentrated in the South East of England, and it is there that rises in employment in this sector have been strongest. Distance from London reduced the speed of growth in this sector, which was lowest, nationally, in Cornwall & West Plymouth. Furthermore, as you move away from London the jobs in this sector tend not to be so well rewarded, growth being in areas such as call-centre employment.

Figure 8.2 Employment in finance in the UK, 1991–2000

Source: UK population Censuses 1991 and 2001, calculated for this book.

The segmentation of employment by financial reward, rather than industrial sector, can be seen by looking at the changing distribution of occupations rather than industry (see Figures 4.10 above and 8.4 below). For now what matters is that it was the finance industry which grew the most in the UK recently. It became ever more concentrated in its historical bastion of London and became a key major source of wealth in the UK. It appeared to support the countries of the UK economically, but was already known in the 1990s also to be increasingly dividing the so-called United Kingdom. Its profits came from extracting interest payments from the rest of the world. What was rarely realised around 2001, but became evident to almost everyone by the end of the 2000s, was that this support was a chimera. Banking and finance quickly came to need everyone else to support it. All those extra jobs were soon to actually make the UK as a whole poorer. It just looked at the time as if the people in white shirts and shiny offices were doing something productive, and few people asked what that something really was and whether what it was leading to was good.

High, rising
Low, rising

Figure 8.3 Employment in elementary occupations in the UK, 1991–2000
Note: Low-paid jobs often described as 'unskilled'.
Source: UK population Censuses 1991 and 2001, calculated for this book.

Figure 8.3 shows that just as employment in the financial industries had risen everywhere in the 1990s, so too has employment in what are termed 'elementary occupations'. These are low-paid jobs deemed by the people who classify jobs to require very little skill to perform, jobs such as cleaning and stacking shelves.

These jobs are fairly evenly distributed across the UK, but their rise in the South is highest in areas a little distant from London, as the people who keep London clean and its shelves stacked with food increasingly have to live further from the capital and have to commute in – a pattern already well established in many North American cities.

Until the crash of 2008, as the population on average became better paid, more skilled, better educated and consumed more, those who could pay increasingly required the services of more and more people in elementary occupations. Around the coast such work may involve caring for the elderly. In rural areas it might be picking flowers or particular vegetables by hand to ensure the (apparent) quality which ever more discerning consumers require. In cities it could be the cleaning of the offices which have replaced declining factories, the serving of fast food and child care for the children of women who are now working. Taken together, this disparate group of occupations, all having in common low pay,

Figure 8.4 Employment in professional occupations in the UK, 1991–2000
Source: UK population Censuses 1991 and 2001, calculated for this book.

were on the increase everywhere, but which particular jobs were on the rise depended on where you were looking. The slowest rise had been in central London. Not because there were not more cleaners in London, but because fewer cleaners lived there and many who did were working at many separate cleaning jobs simultaneously.

At the other end of the pay scale there were also sustained increases in employment in certain sectors in the 1990s – shown in Figure 8.4 as increasing proportions of the population working in professional occupations through to 2001. These are jobs that usually require a university degree and which tend to be well paid. The same proportion of people (4%) worked in professional employment, in 1991, as in elementary occupations, although employment in the former rose by 1% and in the latter by 2% over the course of that 1990s decade.

Soon there were more and more professional jobs clustering in the South, rather than in the North, especially in and around London. They also tended to be better paid in the South, being more common in the private sector and science, rather than in the state-funded health and education services. The fastest rise in professional employment has been in central London and the slowest in South Yorkshire. Thus not only are professionals better paid in the capital, but there are ever more of them going there whereas there tend to be fewer professionals in the North.

In the North the numbers of professionals have been rising more slowly and they tend to work in professions which, although still generously paid, are not as well rewarded as in the South (this is more clearly the case when in the private sector but is also true in much of the public sector as there are more 'senior' public sector posts in the South). It is almost certainly because there is greater demand for their skills in the South, and hence greater rewards there, that this movement is occurring. The source of that increased demand is largely the financial sector and a centralised government and research sector that tends to shadow the financiers' movements.

One way in which demand for labour can be measured is in the number of hours for which people are employed to work. Figure 8.5 shows both the proportion of the population working 31 or more hours a week in 1991 and how that proportion has changed over the course of the 1990s. Although the greatest increases in people working full-time had been in south and central London, the highest proportions were to be found just west and south west of the capital in the most affluent parts of the Home Counties.

Across most of the UK the proportion of people working long hours rose as the demand for their labour appeared to grow, but it is in the South where full-time employment increased more strongly and still remains most common, and it is only in East London that a fall was to be found anywhere in the South prior to 2001. Conversely, in Birmingham East, where manufacturing employment declined the most, and in a scattering of other places across the North, the proportion of the population working these

Figure 8.5 People employed to work full-time in the UK, 1991–2000

Source: UK population Censuses 1991 and 2001, calculated for this book.

hours has fallen as demand for such labour has reduced. It has fallen much more rapidly recently.

The proportion of people working full-time is also reduced where large numbers of people are permanently sick (and that has risen), where many are retired and where there are many children (as all the numbers in these maps are shown as proportions of the entire population). In areas with high numbers of children, elderly, or ill people, many working-age adults have to give many hours a week of unpaid time to care for people who need their care. Thus none of these geographies can be understood in isolation.

Geographical divisions by rates of illness present some of the starkest divides in the UK, and these are reflected by the geography of mortality shown in Chapter 7. Those people who doubt that such large numbers of people really are as sick as they say they are simply need to compare maps of illness with maps of mortality. One such map of illness is shown in Figure 8.6. This is the map of

Figure 8.6 People who are permanently sick in the UK, 1991–2000

Source: UK population Censuses 1991 and 2001, calculated for this book

people who cannot work because they are permanently sick, but who are generally of working age.

From 1991 to 2001 the proportion of the population who were permanently sick rose everywhere, nationally, from 3% to 4% of all people. Outside parts of London and Cornwall, all the areas with above-average rates of permanent sickness in 1991 were in the North of the UK, as the map shading of Figure 8.6 shows. The rates of illnesses could rise as mortality overall fell because more and more of the illnesses were debilitating, but not fatal. Key among all these were rising levels of anxiety and depression as many people became more fearful of the future and of their current situation.

The fastest rise in illness in the 1990s was in Northern Ireland and the slowest was in Surrey. It would be difficult to find two places in the UK which contrast quite so much in so many ways. In Surrey, and most of the areas around it, only 2% of the population were permanently sick by 2001 and there had been only the slightest of increases in that proportion over time. In Northern Ireland the rate rose from 4% to 7% of the entire population in just those ten years, and in other largely urban areas of the North it became as high as 8% or 9% of all people by 2001. If these percentages were expressed as proportions of the working-age populations of these places, they would, of course, be much higher.

High, rising
Low, rising

Figure 8.7 People who are not unemployed in the UK, 1991–2000

Source: UK population Censuses 1991 and 2001, calculated for this book.

Over the course of the 1990s decade, while rates of sickness rose universally, if unevenly, rates of unemployment fell everywhere in the UK. Figure 8.7 shows the inverse of that distribution, the proportion of the population who were not unemployed and how that changed, up to 2001. Children and pensioners cannot be unemployed by census measures and so, once working and otherwise occupied adults were added, everywhere at least 90% of the population fell into this category in 1991 and by 2001 at least 95% of the population of each part of the UK were not unemployed. Put another way, maximum unemployment rates as expressed as a proportion of the entire population fell from 10% to 5% during these ten years. However, those changes were not evenly distributed. Falls in employment never are, as rises in employment tended to be greatest in the recent past where there were most working-age adults available for work.

The largest fall in unemployment in the 1990s was in Glasgow, which also had the highest unemployment rate in 1991. By 2001, Glasgow had the highest proportion of people who were permanently sick in the UK, as the statistics behind Figure 8.6 illustrate. Those used to construct Figure 8.5 showed that it also had the lowest proportion of its population working full-time anywhere in the UK, and those behind Figure 8.1 showed that the city had the smallest workforce employed in manufacturing outside central London. Its population employed in the financial industries did rise quickly from 4% to 7% over these ten years, but in Glasgow that means mainly call-centre work and, since the census was taken, such employment has appeared ever more precarious. The quick fall in unemployment in 1990s Glasgow masks many other changes.

One change, which has been most extreme in places such as Glasgow, has been in the rise in the numbers of people living in lone-parent families where the parent does not have a job. One part of Figure 8.8 is coloured as it is because in Glasgow in the 1990s the proportion of the whole population living in such households rose from 6% to 8% of all people, the majority of these people being children. Thus twice as many people live in lone-parent households with no work as there are unemployed people in Glasgow. Unless you consider the characteristics of the entire population, and all the ways in which they might be economically labelled, you can come to very unrepresentative conclusions by concentrating on just unemployment.

Nationally, 4% of all people in 2001 lived in the kinds of household mapped in Figure 8.8, a rise of 1% in ten years. Nowhere has seen a fall in the size of this group. The smallest increase was in Surrey and the fastest increase in Birmingham East. If you look at the raw data behind these maps you can note how it tends to be the same places that top and tail the ranking of change by many different measures. It is often impossible to bring up children in Surrey if you are a lone parent and have no job. Houses simply cost too much there and there is very little social housing. In contrast, recent industrial decline will have helped to split up more families in Birmingham East in recent years. There is less work for these lone parents and there are more children to be parents of in this area, but housing is cheaper.

In places like Surrey people tend to delay having children until they are older and have established their 'career'. In fact, many people cannot afford to move into the area until they have done so. There are fewer children there, and so there are fewer children to be lone parents of. In contrast, most people who do have children in Surrey tend to be two-parent couples where both parents have to work to be able to afford to live where they do. Thus while high proportions of the children of Birmingham East are deprived of financial resources because the parent they live with does not earn, high proportions of children in Surrey are deprived of time with their parents but not of financial resources.

High, rising
Low, rising

Figure 8.8 Lone parents not in work in the UK, 1991–2000

Source: UK population Censuses 1991 and 2001, calculated for this book.

Figure 8.9 shows the complicated map of both the proportions of people living in two working-parent households, and the change in that proportion over the course of the 1990s. Outside the major cities, more so in the South, the proportion of people living in such households is high and has been growing. Examination of the raw data shows that this is most obviously the case in

West Kent. In urban areas the proportion tends to be lower and it is falling most quickly in North East London, principally because there are fewer families with children there. People are now almost two and a half times more likely to be living in this kind of a family in West Kent as compared to North East London. Thus the very nature of everyday family life has been becoming more polarised geographically by a combination of economic and demographic changes.

Figure 8.9 Two parents both in work in the UK, 1991–2000

Source: UK population Censuses 1991 and 2001, calculated for this book.

Figure 8.10 shows the most stunning of all the social changes to have occurred in recent years in relation to the segmentation of people by labour. This map is of the proportion of (and changes in the number of) people aged 16 or over suffering from a limiting long-term illness or disability. Nationally this ratio rose in the 1990s from 12% to 18% of the population and that change is not due to ageing – a glance at the patterns to the changes best illustrates that. Both changing demographics and economic circumstances do, however, have a part to play in amplifying the growing divisions seen here.

Nowhere are rates of illness falling. They are rising most slowly in the South, and least in London South Inner. They are rising most rapidly in Northern Ireland, but there are also rapidly rising rates in most northern urban areas. In parts of Scotland and Wales over one-quarter of the population are adults with a disability and that level will quickly be reached in many other areas at current rates of change (to soon be double those rates in parts of the South). Less than one-quarter of these people are 'permanently sick and unable to work' (see Figure 8.6). It is thus not an increase in the number of people claiming various benefits which contributes most to this rise.

More and more people in the UK are unable to perform tasks, which limits them, due to illness. Maybe we expect to be able to do more and are frustrated

Figure 8.10   Adults with a long-term illness in the UK, 1991–2000

Source: UK population Censuses 1991 and 2001, calculated for this book.

when we cannot? Maybe we are also recognising that living with an enhanced sense of anxiety is debilitating and that many of us did not suffer from what used to be called 'nerves' as much before? Maybe becoming ever more divided makes us all a little bit more nervous?

AN EXERCISE

Segmentation and polarisation are not simple things to measure and there are no set ways of defining them. Take as an example the ten distributions just described in this chapter. In each case you need to go to the website (see link on www. dannydorling.org) of this book to get the underlying data which provides you with both the proportion of people allocated to each particular group in 1991 and how that proportion has changed in the years to 2001, allowing you to also calculate the number of people so allocated at the end of the period. The website for the first edition of the book, which used very differently presented maps, also has this data shown within each map, and it can be found at www.sasi.group.shef.ac.uk/hguk/ chapter8.htm, which is the web address for the old maps of Chapter 8 of this book.

If you sum the two percentages shown in each area on the old maps, the first versions of these maps to be drawn, then you will find the proportion working in that industry in 2001. All the figures in that on-line map, and in the nine that follow it, are proportions, expressed as percentages, of the entire population. They follow the same format to aid comparison. The versions shown in this book are simpler, just using four shades, but relying on exactly the same data. Whichever way you access it, you end up with ten sets of data, and each set containing two times 85 statistics. Although the numbers are only provided as whole percentages, without having this dataset on computer there are too many distributions to consider for any one person, therefore each select one of the ten distributions to study.

If there are 20 or more of you, you can each also select a year to study, either 1991 or 2001 (although the first and fourth methods defined below allow you to consider both years simultaneously). You need to determine how spatially polarised people were in the year you are looking at for the variable you are considering. There are many ways in which you can do this; some are listed below. Agree a method among yourselves, perhaps more than one, calculate the degree of polarisation which has occurred and then read on. Here are some methods you can use:

1   Most simply, you can say a variable is polarising over time if the majority of areas fall into the shading categories: low and falling or high and rising. However, some variables are rising in every area or falling everywhere. In those cases you can subtract the national average (say median) change from the change measured first, and then redefine every place as either rising or falling as compared to national changes. Work out the median change simply by writing down the changes in order and selecting the middle, 43rd, one.

2 You can measure the degree of segregation of a group at a given time. For instance, what proportion of people in these countries would have to move between areas for that group to be evenly distributed across the UK? Or what proportion of the group would have to move, or what number of people would have to move, or what number or proportion would have to move if that group were to be distributed as evenly or unevenly everybody *not* in that group is? You have a lot of options as to how to calculate just these simple measures of segregation.

3 You can measure the chances of someone chosen at random from the group you are studying meeting another person from the same group if that person were also chosen at random from within their area. This is called an isolation index and is easier to calculate than to describe (it is simply the sums of all the proportions weighted by those proportions, as you can assume each area has equal population). One problem for this index is that it tends to be higher the larger the size of a group is nationally. Can you correct for that?

4 You can work out some average changes and draw a histogram of the results. For instance, in areas (grouped) which had a high proportion of people in a group in 1991, what has the average change in their numbers been? What about for average areas, below average areas and so on? For each type of area, as defined by proportion in 1991, there will have been an average change, which you can calculate. You can draw a histogram of those changes. If the tails of the histogram tend to rise and the centre falls, then polarisation has occurred. But what if the pattern is more complex than that?

5 Think up your own way of measuring polarisation or segmentation and change in those measures. Ideally your measure should be simple to understand and preferably simple to calculate. It should measure something which is meaningful, its size should mean something and changes in its size should be readily interpretable. Can you think of a better way of describing whether the patterns shown in the maps above really do represent growing cleavages in the human geography of society or whether the changes are not as dramatic as that?

Having measured the levels of polarisation or segmentation in whichever way you have chosen, and having looked at the change over time in those measures, you next need to interpret the results. What has been going on? How would you explain your findings to an audience similar to yourselves? Can you appreciate why I have not included such measures here – or would their inclusion have altered the story being told in the chapter above? Should I have included such measures?

Having done all this work, what criticisms would you make of this chapter of the book? Can you tell simply from looking at the maps how the countries of the UK are changing? Is the UK becoming a more or less divided place, at least by what these measures show? And finally, why consider these measures? What really matters most about places in people's lives?

Conclusion

The population of the UK has become more segmented by the kinds of work people do, the rewards for that work and the outcomes of those growing spatial divisions. Underlying these changes is the continued decline of traditional industries, and most recently the bailing out of much of the finance sector, which has further exacerbated the geographical divides revealed above. Foremost among the declining traditional industries, still in terms of the numbers of people involved, is manufacturing.

In 2001, for the first time ever, manufacturing employed fewer people than the financial industries, and these shifts had profound geographical outcomes. The UK has been transformed from an island in which the majority of people farmed or fished, to a set of countries in which manufacturing was the occupation of the majority, to a nation state in which the largest employment sector concerns the movement of other people's monies. The bulk of the jobs, and certainly the best paid jobs in this sector, are in the South of England, especially in London. It is thus to London that the most skilled young labour now travels (as we define skills today). It is in and around London that there has been the greatest increase in professional employment, where more and more people are working longer hours, where more children are growing up in households where both adults work, where sickness and unemployment are most rare.

More people are also engaged in the most elementary of occupations as a result of the changes revealed here. There is growing demand for people to be employed to do work which in the recent past we would have done for ourselves. We (the rich) now expect, and are willing to pay for, someone else to make coffee for us in a shop, for there to be millions more metres of shelf space in other shops for us to browse along when we choose what to spend our increased earnings on. All those shelves have to be filled. We increasingly expect other people to care for our children in the day when we are at work and to look after our parents when they age (rather than let them live with us).

Given the huge rise in menial jobs, greater even than that in professional employment, it is hardly surprising that more people are ill. Add to that the rising numbers who have no job because the industries they used to work in have shut down, and who do not possess the qualifications or youthfulness to work in the new industries, and then add to that the rising numbers of people struggling to bring up children on their own without a wage while others have more money than they need for their children, and it would be disingenuous to suggest that this rise in illness were artificial. Then add rising youth unemployment.

Illness rates have risen most where people are poorest, where rates were highest to begin with and where the majority of people live who die prematurely. This rise in illness has not been translated into a lowering of life expectancies except for in a very few small areas and for a few social groups; it is not a rise in terminal physical maladies therefore. The rising rates of illness are not killing more people, although they do provide part of the explanation as to why inequalities in mortality have continued to rise over the course of the 1990s and through to at least the early 2000s, and most probably to the present day.

The patterns shown here suggest that the bulk of the massive rise in illness in the UK is socially induced: reactions to the growing inequalities in life in these countries. These inequalities affect people's lives, their abilities to cope with problems, the quality and speed of treatment and the support they receive, depending on where they live and the nature of any specific illness or disability.

Those least affected by their local environments – the wealthy and able – are, ironically, those most likely to be able to move to avoid living in an area they perceive as limiting. The same people are most able to change who they are in ways which suit the vagaries of employment. Thus the growth in finance has not been caused by a transfer from manufacturing employment of people who would have otherwise worked in that. It has required migration to occur because the two sectors are not generally located in the same places. Furthermore, they do not generally employ the same people.

Many more women work in finance than in manufacturing. A degree is of little use when it comes to actually making things but is apparently essential to being well rewarded in an investment bank or insurance company. The changing industrial geography of the UK is altering the geographies of occupation, the demographic profile of areas, how families are brought up and where, and overall states of health. And there is no reason to assume that this process is likely to be reversed in the near future. Even the most calamitous banking crash resulted in far more hardship in areas with little banking as compared to the areas where the banks were major employers.

Where there are increases in the proportions of people working in manufacturing it tends to be in places where cottage and small-scale industries are more common. Universities are producing ever more graduates to feed the appetite of the southern labour market. Some graduates will work in call centres, but if they do so they will displace others who could have worked in those jobs and by doing so are going to increase inequalities in employment. However, more and more graduates can find no work as even the financial sector is hiring fewer new starters. More will look to move overseas. We should also expect many more young adults to become either angry or depressed or a mixture of both.

Freed from the nineteenth- and early twentieth-century reliance on the physical resources of particular areas for particular industries, buoyant, financially secure and successful companies are more able, in theory, to choose where they locate. But they want to locate within reasonable distance of an able workforce, for their workers to be able to travel easily to where they need to go to carry out that work, to be near large international airports and other amenities of a capital, and they want a housing market in which the high salaries they can afford to pay can compete. Given all this, the finance industry is bound to concentrate in the South. Peripheral activities, back offices, call centres, clearing warehouses can be sited outside, but only if they can easily be moved to other locations in the future.

In Bristol, Leeds and Edinburgh there are regional offshoots of the major London institutions, but these are simply half-way houses of decentralisation within easy train or plane distance of the capital. They also hardly feature as significant on the national map of this industry. Most importantly, when you can partly choose where to locate your industry, then why place it among the decaying remnants of former industries in areas suffering all the problems of depopulation, illness and worklessness that result?

The rise of the car, of working at home, and the repopulation of the centre of the capital have all made more space for the expansion of the finance industries in the South. They have also helped in increasing the segmentation of the labour market and the social polarisation of areas. If there were not a continued and growing demand for unskilled labour – by those who are paid the most – there would be no poor areas in the South of England, especially in London. Exorbitant incomes are of little use if they do not buy you luxuries, and the biggest luxury of all is not having to do things for yourself. Thus even within the South of England we see spatial divisions grow, as they widen too with the North.

For spatial divisions to fall social income and wealth inequalities would have to fall, and expectations adjust accordingly. Currently we are served in shops and cafés by the tenth of the population who now work there. The more money we have the more we are served. In the not too distant future it is conceivable that we will begin seeing servants 'living in' again. In some parts of London this has already begun.

Further Reading

Here is a report from a Citizens' Advice Bureau written as long ago as 1998 about a woman who could not work:

> Mrs. J has arthritis in her spine and knees, and asthma. She was found fit for work so incapacity benefit stopped. She appealed and signed on for Jobseeker's Allowance to avoid the 20% reduction in benefit. She found a job, worked two weeks, couldn't cope physically, started a different job, worked three weeks, had to give up, couldn't cope again, started third job, gives up. By now the linking period allowing a break of 8 weeks in entitlement to incapacity benefit without penalty was broken. So despite the fact that the appeal was successful and she was found again to be unfit for work she had to start again with a new claim for incapacity benefit at a lower rate.
>
> (to read further, see www.informedcompassion.com)

If each of her new jobs were recorded as the creation of some new work, and if each time she left a new vacancy was recorded, for this one person, in such a short time, how many jobs and vacancies have been created, all by this one woman's misfortune? Now have a look at this website of official unemployment and vacancy data and try to work out what the numbers really mean: http:// timetric.com/topic/labour-vacancies-uk-ons-data/.

Key Point Summary

- There has been a polarisation in UK industry with finance rising and manu-facturing falling.

- There have also been more better-paid jobs created, and more work that is menial in nature.

- The most recent economic downturn has tended to reinforce previously established trends.

9

HOME

... the settlements of society

People's lives in the UK are most influenced day to day by how they are settled and housed – what it is like where they are living. The patterns to housing and settlement are long established yet they are also slowly changing in response to people's changing migration patterns, educational changes, changing social identities, new housing policies/politics, growing economic inequalities, ageing and illness, and the changing industrial and occupational geographies of the UK.

This chapter begins by considering how closely together or sparsely spaced people are, where major settlements have their greatest demographic influences and how those patterns are changing. Following these considerations we turn to the way these changes have altered the types of housing people are living in, then what kinds of household live where – according to their economic position – and how they pay for their housing as a result.

The wealth that can be accumulated through housing is our next focus, and also the attributes of some people's houses and lives which reflect that wealth, where many people live in large houses or with access to many other material goods. Finally, the chapter looks at where most ill and very elderly people live, including those who have to care for others in their neighbourhood and how people are cared for when friends and family are not able to, or are no longer willing to, provide that care.

People in the UK are housed in many different ways and live in an ever widening variety of different types of household and family, although increasing numbers are also living alone. The types of housing and households people live in are strongly influenced not only by their economic, demographic and social circumstances but also by where they live. In some parts of the UK there is very little space per person and even the affluent live cheek by jowl in the densest of city centres (where living alone is an expensive luxury). In other areas, particularly where the population has been declining, there is a general surplus of housing, although few people in such areas can afford to build large homes. Collected together, homes form settlements, areas that people have settled, usually for centuries.

The structures of British settlements are changing slowly; their nature is
changing more quickly. In earlier chapters we considered in more detail the
nature of different groups of people living in different areas and how they came
to be there, how they are changing the places they live in, how they express their
content or discontent through political behaviour, how their lives are economically and socially inequitable, how this translates into patterns seen in their
deaths and how the changing demands for their skills, abilities and time are
altering all these pictures. Here we end our tour of the UK by considering how
we are looked after in terms of the most basic need we have – shelter – how
some are better housed than others and how the pattern of our settlement of this
land is changing as a result.

Britain is a very unevenly populated landmass. It is often said to be a
crowded island, yet most of the land is only sparsely settled. Figure 9.1 is a map

≥ 40
30 to 40
20 to 30
10 to 20
< 10

Figure 9.1 Population density in the UK, 2001

Source: UK population Census 2001, calculated for this book as population-weighted density
(local authorities are base units).

of the average population densities at which people lived in each area of the UK in 2001. This is an average of the densities for each local authority area within each of the areas. It better reflects population density as perceived by the inhabitants of each area than does the simple ratio of people to land. The measure varies from over 100 people per hectare in central London (1 person per 10 x 10 metres square), to 0.2 people per hectare in the Highlands & Islands of Scotland (1 person per 250 x 250 metres square).

Figure 9.2 Population potential in the UK, 2001

Source: UK population Census 2001, calculated for this book as the population per metre away from each local authority to every other, and a population-weighted mean calculated for each area shown.

It is often said that in much of Britain people are never more than a few metres away from the rats which live in the sewers. In central London most people are never much more than 10 metres away from the next human being. The population of this island is most concentrated along a diagonal line which runs from Glasgow down through sparsely populated areas along the west coast main railway line, through Manchester to Birmingham, ending in London. They are there because that is where most of the housing was built in the past. This is becoming increasingly the main reason for current settlement the further north you travel. In England, most people in the South live at lower densities than do the population of the North, bar the crowding of the capital. The housing in the North was built for higher-density living.

The diagonal axis of population in Britain is made ever more evident when, instead of considering population density, we consider population potential – how many people are near each person (Figure 9.2). Population potential is simply calculated by summing the population of the UK, with the contribution of each part of that sum being weighted by the distance to the place you are calculating it for. It is expressed as the average number of people per metre away from any

Figure 9.3 Change in population potential in the UK, 1991–2001

Source: UK population Censuses 1991 and 2001, population potential calculated for this book by local authority (see Figure 9.3), 1991 statistics substracted from 2001 and a population-weighted mean shown.

point. It creates a surface which peaks in central London where it reaches highs of over 1000 'people per metre away' within the centre of the capital.

At its lowest in mainland Britain, population potential stands at just over 100 in the far north of Scotland. Put another way, and given that the population of the mainland in 2001 was roughly 58 million, then (very roughly) half the population in Britain lives 580 km from the North of Scotland, but only 58 km from London. The higher an area's population potential, the easier it is for more people to visit there, the greater will be its labour and consumer markets in volume, the higher will be demand for land and space within the area, and the population will tend to be more crowded.

Had we included the population of Europe or the world in this calculation, and skewed their distance to each place to be calculated as passing through the major airports, then the pattern would be very much more concentrated in the capital than it appears even from this map. Northwest London is found towards the centre of Britain. It just appears to be near the edge.

Figure 9.3 plots the change that has occurred in population potential over the course of the 1990s. The changes are of, at most, only a few dozen or so extra people per metre, although what appear to be tiny reductions in this measure of people have implications which are critical for the population of the UK, and for the changing fortunes of the places we live in.

The population is rising in the South, centred on a peak of growth in the capital, and is falling in the North West, North East, and parts of Scotland. It is those changes which create the very smooth pattern of overall change seen in Figure 9.3. As to the importance of these changes to housing: imagine that the supply of housing is largely fixed, a little is built and demolished each year, but there is ever less space to build homes where people most want them. It is largely restrictions on such building which has kept much of the South at low housing densities. Imagine next that the authorities are reluctant to demolish homes given the cost of building them and the effect such demolition without rebuilding can have on areas. Thus, as the stock of homes is largely fixed, when populations fall their value falls even faster and when there are slight increases in the pressure to live in popular areas this is greatly amplified through rises in the cost of housing in those areas. There are many reasons why the population is changing in the directions shown here. What matters here are the implications of these long-term migratory, mortality and local fertility shifts.

Just one example of the effect of population movement can be seen in terms of the changing proportion of people housed in flats, as shown in Figure 9.4. Few flats are built each decade. The population in flats mostly increases because three people live in a flat rather than two, or two rather than one. Similarly, outside Glasgow, which has seen many flats demolished (and hence a 15% fall in the proportion of its residents living in such accommodation in the 1990s alone), the main reason why the population living in flats is reducing is that where in the past two people lived in a flat, now one does.

In general in Britain where the population is falling, increasing proportions of the people who are left live in houses; and where the population is rising, increasing proportions will live in flats. This is one of the simplest examples of how overall settlement change in Britain is altering the way people are housed on this island. The rising popularity of living in flats is not simply confined to the capital, but can be found across the South East of England in almost exactly those same places where population potential is rising most quickly. In much of the South East people live at relatively low densities. Thus it is not lack of land which is constraining more and more people to live in flats here. A combination of factors, from the price of housing, to the need to be near railway stations, to the restrictions placed on new building by the authorities, all play a part.

Figure 9.4   Change in the proportion of people living in flats, 1991–2001
Source: UK population Censuses 1991 and 2001, calculated for this book.

The type of housing people can afford to live in is as strongly influenced by their ability to pay for it as by what is available to buy or rent, and what is being provided by the state and its agencies. Figure 9.5 shows areas of Britain typified by the main economic activity of adults in each area. As with the figures shown in Chapter 4, this map is not of what is most usual, but of what group is most over-represented as compared to the national average distribution of these people in Britain. This form of mapping is used to make the spatial differences more easily distilled within a single image.

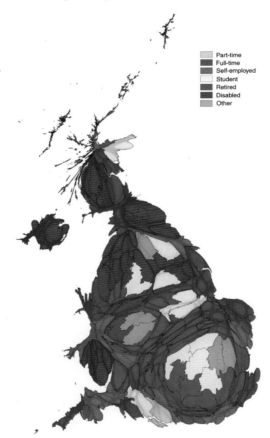

Part-time
Full-time
Self-employed
Student
Retired
Disabled
Other

Figure 9.5 People by dominant economic activity in the UK, 2001

Note: Most unusually large group is shown when each place is compared with the UK.

Source: Analysis of the 2001 Census Key Statistics by local authority.

Figure 9.5 shows that much of the North, Wales, Scotland and Northern Ireland houses more people suffering from a disability than is the norm, and that difference in over-representation is greater for this group than for any other group in the area. In Glasgow, for example, there are 6.7% more such people than in the UK as a whole and that 6.7% difference is greater than the next largest discrepancy (there being 2.5% more students among the population of

Glasgow than the average share of students in each area, a secondary fact which cannot easily be shown by this kind of mapping).

In contrast to the North, the South has a large cluster of areas typified by having unusually large proportions of their populations working full-time. Between these extremes there are many other patterns to people's economic status, as shown in Figure 9.5, but this map is one of the keys to understanding how people come to be housed differently across the UK.

Owner
Mortgage
Local Authority
Housing Association
Private rented

Figure 9.6 Tenure of households in the UK, 1991–2001

Note: Most unusually large group is shown when each place is compared with the UK.

Source: Analysis of the 2001 Census Key Statistics by local authority.

The past distribution of homes, the supply of land and the economic status of households are some of the most important key factors in understanding how people come to pay for their housing. But, for understanding the map of tenure shown in Figure 9.6, a fourth factor has to be included – demography. One-third of the population own their home outright. Most of these people are old and, as the figure shows, they are disproportionately distributed around the coast. To have owned their home, most will have had a mortgage, usually on a different property initially and sometimes in a different area.

Mortgages are the most common form of tenure in the Home Counties. Most people who take out a mortgage rent privately before doing so and renting is the typical atypical (i.e. unusually large) tenure of much of London. Private renting is, however, the most expensive form of tenure in the long run and many people cannot afford it. Much private rented stock is also only suitable for young childless adults.

One-fifth of all households are housed by local councils or housing associations where the state or its agents are the landlord. This tenure is most typical of the North of England, Northern Ireland and Scotland, although social housing is also over-represented in three areas of London. Compare the

Figure 9.7   Households with seven or more rooms in the UK, 2001

Source: UK population Census 2001, calculated for this book.

map of how people pay for or own their homes against the map of what people do in the economy, the maps of age structure and other identities shown in Chapter 4, of how people vote (in Chapter 5), of what they earn (in Chapter 6) and of how they die (in Chapter 7).

Homes, of course, differ not only in how they are paid for and how they are built, but in what you get for your money and your land. Figure 9.7 shows the proportions of people who live in homes with seven or more main rooms in them. These are generally the most expensive properties in each area, but in some areas almost one-third of all homes are as large as this. Where people already have a kitchen, dining room and sitting room on the ground floor and three bedrooms above them, the addition of a single extra bedroom through building an extension will bring a home into this category (toilets and other small rooms are not counted here).

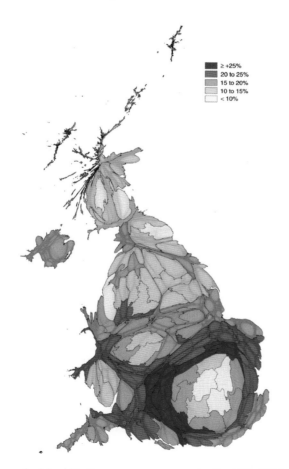

Figure 9.8 Households with three or more cars in the UK, 2001

Source: UK population Census 2001, calculated for this book.

Seven-or-more-room houses are most rare in Glasgow, despite the recent demolition of so many flats there. Next it is within London that fewest are found, despite the immense amount of money flowing through the capital. Where there is either lack of money or lack of space, such housing is rare. It is most commonly found in the South, although the proportions of large properties to be found in rural Wales and Northern Ireland are high. However, a large proportion of those in Wales will be owned by people who have retired from England. People who are retired need no longer live within commuting distances of major workplaces. Moving towards where land and properties are cheaper allows some to buy larger and more comfortable homes than they could have lived in when working in England. It also results in some people working in Wales having to live in smaller homes than they otherwise would.

The tenure of housing, its type, worth and how large it is, tells us some aspects of how people are housed but not much about what is actually within those walls – what possessions people own or have access to in their household. Many surveys are made of these but few result in information which can easily be mapped, even at the crude level used in this book. One thing that is consistently asked in population censuses and which does have a great influence on housing is how many cars, if any, each household has access to.

Figure 9.8 above shows the proportion of households that have access to three or more cars. It is a strikingly similar distribution to that of rooms, albeit with fewer cars in retirement areas where more households consist of just one or two people, some too infirm to drive or who never had a driving license. Again, rates in West Wales are similar to Northern Ireland. The two areas in the Home Counties where 31% of people live in homes with seven or more rooms also see 31% of their households having access to three or more cars.

It is partly through owning so many cars that affluent middle-aged people have managed such a take-over of the Home Counties, which only a few decades ago were rural enclaves rather than commuter settlements. They also have space to house the cars as well as the money to afford to buy and run them. In the cities there is simply not the parking space on roads for so many cars per household; and there are other forms of transport available, especially in London, and so we see a clear urban/suburban divide here. In fact, cars per person were falling in London during the 1990s and are probably still falling as more people squeeze in but cannot park their cars and often do not really need them in that city.

Car ownership tends to be lower in the North even where there is space to park vehicles, and in rural areas where cars might be considered more of a necessity. People in the North of England spend less time in cars partly because more of them cannot afford to drive so much. They also have other calls on their time. Figure 9.9 shows how it is in the North, Wales, Northern Ireland and much of Scotland that people are most likely to have to give up 50 or more hours a week caring for a relative or neighbour who is ill or

infirm, while the South is dominated by areas where what is most disproportionately high are the numbers of people who do not need to provide any
such care.

Figure 9.9 The landscape of unpaid care for the ill in the UK, 2001

Note: Most unusually large group is shown when each place is compared with the UK (there
are no areas with 20 to 49 hours).

Source: Analysis of the 2001 Census Key Statistics by local authority.

Although rich and poor can be found everywhere, there are increasingly two
Britains. In one, at the extreme, you will find homes within which two adults
work and are well rewarded, where everyone has a bedroom to themselves and
even the teenager has his or her own car, where mum and dad have almost paid
off the mortgage and have seen the value of their property double several times
since they first moved in. In contrast, at the other extreme, you will find smaller

homes where a single elderly and infirm person lives, whose daughter visits often to look after her or him. Such people have no car and no capital as they pay their rent to the council, and when their neighbours die, every so often no one new moves in, these areas are mostly in the North. And this gap has been growing from both two decades before, and ever since, the data in these maps was collected, almost a dozen years ago.

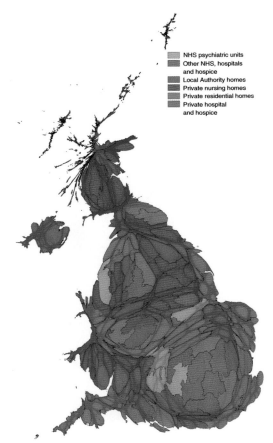

Figure 9.10   Institutional care in old age and illness in the UK, 2001

Note: Most unusually large group is shown when each place is compared with the UK.

Source: Analysis of the 2001 Census Key Statistics by local authority.

Figure 9.10, the final map of this chapter, is one possible depiction of where most people end up being housed towards the end of their lives and how that currently differs across the UK. The map is of the population who live in the institutions, hospitals or the various 'homes' which are listed. The most atypically populous type of accommodation is shown, rather than the most common, to highlight the geographical patterns.

London and much of the non-coastal south is unusual in that in these places relatively high numbers of people are found in NHS or private hospitals and hospices. These show up here mainly because the other institutional populations are so low in these areas. In practice hospitals mostly cater for a population which moves in and out of them rapidly.

From the Welsh border all around the southern coast to Lincolnshire an almost uninterrupted swathe of private *care* homes dominate. In the North, Wales, Scotland and Northern Ireland it is private *nursing* homes that are more typical. Often the authorities pay for people to be housed in these when they can no longer cope at home and need medical care. Care homes are more of a luxury, often for the children of the elderly – who then need not care for their parents. There are far fewer private care homes in the North of England and in Scotland, Wales and Northern Ireland.

AN EXERCISE

Try to imagine how the UK might look if this book were to be rewritten in 50 years' time. Today's university leavers will be of pensionable age, but which will have good pensions? Where will they have moved to, and how will they be accommodated? Many of their parents will still be alive if life expectancy continues to rise as it has done for the last 50 years, but who will be caring for them? There will be fewer people of working age and fewer children again, unless today's school leavers behave differently from their parents or unless more young people come into the UK than leave it.

In 2062 of what will the housing stock be made up? How many of the Victorian terraces will still be standing? What will be the state of the homes built around the middle of the last century, now all at least a century old? And will some families still have the state or its agents as their landlords? Which settlements will have declined and which will have grown? Will the old still move to the coast? Will the young still cluster in university towns and move in large numbers to the capital? Will fewer or more people be ill? Of what will the population now be dying? What could the human geography of the UK look like in the future. Will there even be a 'United' Kingdom then?

Speculation over the future is a fraught but interesting exercise. One way to conduct it is to divide your speculation up by how uncertain you are about different issues. Start with issues you think are more certain, move on to things which are more uncertain, and end with pure speculation. To start you off here is one possible way in which you could begin with a set of issues to consider:

1 *More certain:* We largely rely now on infrastructure built over 50 years ago – roads, rail, sewers and houses. Thus we largely live in the same places we lived in half a century ago. What is the state of this infrastructure? What kinds of things could you expect to see built in the coming years? For

example, airports often take decades to plan and build. High-speed rail tracks can take even longer. What might the impact of such changes be?

2 *Less certain:* Some aspects of human life change slowly and in one direction for long periods of time, for example the fall in fertility, the rise in life expectancy, people being educated for longer and longer periods, national wealth rising, inequalities not tending to diminish. If those aspects of life in the UK which have changed slowly and in a steady direction for most of the last 50 years were to continue on their way, what would the future hold for us? What if you include trends which appear to be cyclical such as economic recessions and, perhaps, fertility?

3 *Pure speculation:* Most forecasts of the future appear to work until something unusual occurs, and there are many unusual things which can occur. The population of the UK was last altered significantly by a major infectious disease pandemic and a war over 90 years ago. How would we cope with such an event in the future? We were last on the receiving end of a major war over 50 years ago. War has far from ended around the globe, so what if we were at war at home again? Both over 100 and 60 years ago radical governments took power in the UK and instigated many changes to improve people's lives. Could that happen again? And what could happen that you have not thought of?

Having thought up a set of issues and characterised them into the three groups above, set to work on outlining possible scenarios for the future, and divide the work up. Draw possible maps of the future. These are far easier to draw than are maps of the present because you can simply make the data up. All you need is for your map to be plausible. For instance, draw a map of the results of a fictional general election in 2062. What kinds of political party might there be and what voting system? Will some children now be allowed to vote or will voting rights be more restricted than today? You may think it unlikely that there will be such elections in 50 years time; after all, elections in which almost all adults are allowed to vote are less than a century old in the UK and there have been only just over two dozen of them, hardly a long time-series. But even if you think like this, try to draw a map of how the alternative to elections might operate.

The one thing you can be (quite) sure of is that there will still be a distinct geographical pattern to the lives of people on and around this island and its province. There always has been. Perhaps the hardest future to imagine is one in which every place becomes more similar to every other as the people living there are concerned. You could move around the UK but you could not tell where you were from, what the people there were doing, how they were living and what they had. It is a difficult future to imagine unless, that is, you were a child of the late 1970s and early 1980s in the UK. Then, if you had believed the rhetoric of government, there would be equality in the future. The poor would grow rich on the trickle-down of monies from the affluent, state housing would all be sold to its inhabitants and the future would be a rosy, prosperous hard-working utopia for all, even for the inhabitants of '*those inner cities*' for which they had '*task forces*'.

In secret, government minsters planned for the 'managed decline' of parts of the North such as Liverpool. This was only revealed 30 years later in January 2012 when cabinet minutes for 1981 were declassified. If you believed some of the opposition to the government of those days, then the future was to be equally equitable if a little more bleak. The opposition said that the government was trying to manage the decline of much of the UK outside of South East England (and that now appears to have been the case). Much more seriously, some parts of the opposition warned that with America's aid we would manage to engage in a nuclear war. Most of us would be killed and the survivors would 'envy the dead'. If this occurred then there would be little variation in the remaining conditions of living across the Kingdom (which would almost certainly no longer be a kingdom), although you'd be well situated if you could get to the Caledonian canal, which would have become the major new trade route for a rapidly emerging new stone age.

Safe to say neither of those predictions came true. The Labour opposition came to power and it said that we would live with greater equality in the future, as government would 'bring Britain back together again', but few believed they would. A kind of peace did come to Northern Ireland, but if you believed other voices, including the barely concealed voice of parts of the government, then what we had most to fear was a bomb or a virus, no longer from the Russians, but still hitting our major cities. In fact, what we had most to fear turned out to be what was being most celebrated. The supposed success story of the financial wizardry of London bankers turned out to be a bomb of a different kind, one which blew up the national finances in 2008.

As I write this we are told that there will soon be a 'Big Society' and people will come together again with a little encouragement from central government to help each other out more often. There is always speculation that somehow we are on a particular road to some kind of a utopia and in some ways it doesn't change a great deal – the authors and actors are altered but the scenes portrayed remain much the same. Unless I am extremely lucky, I won't be around to see what the world looks like in 2062. For my generation and older folk, your predictions cannot be proved right or wrong.

Conclusion

How we are housed, from when we are born through to where we die, produces patterns on the maps of life in the UK which reflect a great amount about us and how we have settled these countries. In the UK almost everyone is given shelter, but the shelter they receive varies greatly and it almost certainly varies more across the countries than it has ever done. To the North are the old industrial cities where the stock of small, often nineteenth-century, housing is ageing. To the South many more homes were built in the last century and far more of these have been enlarged and modernised than in the North.

For over a century the population of the UK has been moving southwards. In recent years large numbers of people have begun moving (net) into London again, which for many decades before 1980 had been becoming less crowded. However, those now moving to London are bringing money or qualifications which they hope will gain them future wealth – but no amount of money can create more space. Thus in the capital even the very rich have to squeeze into smaller and smaller spaces.

In the 1990s in London the numbers of people having access to cars declined. Saturation point for the parking of vehicles was reached while the population continued to grow. There are probably again today fewer cars per person in London than there were a decade ago. In contrast, around London the population is still relatively sparsely distributed. Strict planning controls, very high land prices and problems of commuting mean that populations have grown far more slowly around the capital as compared to within it. However, many of those who can live in the Home Counties have quietly added rooms and wings to their properties, increasing their value further.

In many places there are almost as many cars as adults – another saturation point has been reached as there are so few left who could drive (people with driving licences and no car). People here are finishing off purchasing their houses, and further out the majority have done so. This is where the housing wealth of the UK is accumulating most clearly. There are exceptions to these generalisations, pockets of poverty in the South, but outside the poorest parts of London such pockets are shrinking, and mile upon mile of land is becoming much the same in terms of who can now live there.

Around the coast of the southern half of the UK are increasingly found the parents of the people who have just paid off their mortgages. These pensioners are living in care homes which are often paid for from the proceeds of their own house sales in the past. Their grandchildren will only be able to buy where they once lived if the grandparents help them. In contrast, in the North, this cycle of money begetting money, of house prices ever rising, of ever increasing demand to settle is found to be far more muted. It is possible that recent house price falls outside of the South of England will spread southwards, but for now the UK continues to polarise, and house prices are still rising rapidly within London (as I correct the proofs to these pages in July 2012).

In parts of the North small areas are being abandoned and larger places depopulated. In many areas there is an elderly population living in flats with too few people to replace them when they leave. In general they will not leave until the state pays for them to enter a nursing home or they die. It is also in the North, in this kind of a housing market, where most people too sick to work are found, where the state and its agents still own large amounts of local housing, where there are far fewer large homes and far fewer families with more vehicles than they need. It is in the North too that the highest numbers of people need to devote the longest time to the unpaid care of others. The very last of the dark satanic mills have finally closed, but the green and pleasant land of the UK is only for the few who can afford it.

Further Reading

Compare a series of British newspapers and also television channel websites. Only bother with ones which have free access. Beware anyone trying to sell you things over the Web. As I write, among those newspapers which are still at least partly free to view on the web are:

www.telegraph.co.uk
www.guardian.co.uk
www.mirror.co.uk
www.thesun.co.uk

There are also other websites which allow further reading that are not so obviously linked to commercial journalism. These include: www.opendemocracy. net, www.socialistreview.org.uk or the blogs of individual writers such as www. monbiot.com and many more. They tend to be a little more interesting than the websites of official statistical agencies, or academic bodies interested in studying demography. Compare these seven sources of information and see what they suggest about the shape of things to come.

Key Point Summary

- Britain is metaphorically tilting, people are leaving the North West, moving into the South.

- People in the South and Wales are more likely to be buying their home or to own it outright.

- You are more likely to end up in a private nursing home in your final days in the South.

10

ABROAD

... the Kingdom's place in the world

From speculating on the future, to trying to understand the present and recent past of the population of the UK, a wider view of the world is required. It is unlikely that the future maps of the human geography of these countries will be largely determined from within, as neither the current nor the past maps have been. The world outside the UK has been ignored in these pages so far, but its influence is clear to see through almost every figure, pattern and event described. The basic map used in these pages is of areas which were created for the election of members of the European Parliament (Figure 1.2) and yet almost nothing has been said on the rest of Europe.

One of the first social landscapes shown on the underlying population-based map used throughout this book was of young adults' chances of entering university (Figure 1.5). The main reason those chances are historically high is that British governments have been trying to catch up with American and other western enrolment rates; the rush to educate was not internally inspired (Figure 1.6). The numbers of people living in these countries and the variation in their ages are products of the two World Wars and other international events (Figure 2.1). Our graduates increasingly flock to London to directly or indirectly serve international financial institutions (Figure 3.10), as do many people from the rest of the world (Figure 4.8).

For those trying to understand why more and more of us do not bother to vote (Figure 5.6), the rising international disillusionment with such participation might help explain that such trends are not purely home grown, neither are the increasing variations in our incomes (Figure 6.2), as recorded by international banks which 'invest' our money around the globe. We can easily see how rates of some diseases depend on external factors (Figure 7.2), but it is international markets that move people around Britain over decades, rewarding some areas and depleting others of resources that result in such stark geographical divides in the ways most of us die (compare Figures 8.2 and 7.7), and which is slowly altering our basic pattern of settlement across this land (Figure 9.3).

The rest of the world has a far greater impact on us than we now have on it. It is the place from where we make our profits, allowing us to generally live a good life, from where much of our food and most of what else we consume comes, it is often because of economic competition with the rest of the world that our politicians tell us we have to work harder and longer and the apparent need for ever more fierce competition is listed as the reason why politicians suggest they cannot easily afford to remedy inequalities within our borders. However, social inequalities within our borders are as nothing compared to those now seen across the globe. Both our distant imperial past and recent world banker re-emergence have helped to foster these divisions.

In this chapter the story of the population of the UK is brought to a close by looking at where that Kingdom now sits in the world. Because this book began by looking at the life chances of children in Britain, it ends by looking at the chances of children across the globe, and at how the UK sits within a far greater map of human population. This is partly a map of the future as it is these children who will determine the fate of the children of our islands in the long term. How does the world look when drawn to depict the lives and chances of its children? How does the UK fit within that map? What is abroad?

The world as viewed by its children is a world dominated by Africa, India and China. The United States of America and Russia are relatively insignificant. The UK is separated by oceans and rich nations from the immediate lives of most of the world's children. Its child population is less than half the size of Egypt, Ethiopia or the Philippines. It is less than one-quarter the size of Nigeria, Brazil or Bangladesh, less than one-fifth the size of Pakistan or Indonesia, and there are almost 30 children in both China and India for each child living in the UK. This is the current map; the future map sees these disparities in population rapidly widening.

When compared with such inequities across the globe, social inequalities in life chances, in access to education, in work and in health within the UK pale into insignificance. However, much the same forces which divide up children's chances geographically within one affluent kingdom are also at play worldwide. People are of different monetary value depending on where and to whom they were born both within Britain and within the world. The results can be dire where there are more people than markets appear to require, and increasing numbers of people rapidly move around the world to avoid such consequences.

Currently world population stands at 7 billion. Most of the children shown in the population maps below are now becoming young adults. As the lives of these children, as adults, are played out during this century, what happens to them will greatly influence what happens to the children of Britain in not too many years to come. Up to this point in these pages it is as if we have been speculating on the state and future of a rich neighbourhood while ignoring the city in which it sits. If the world were a city, the UK would be an affluent neighbourhood offset from the core of that city, but ever less immune from its future, its rapid growth, its claims for fairer resources, and the abject poverty in many of the other neighbourhoods.

What most clearly divides the world's children is the poverty many are growing up in as compared to the affluence of most of those living in the rich nations

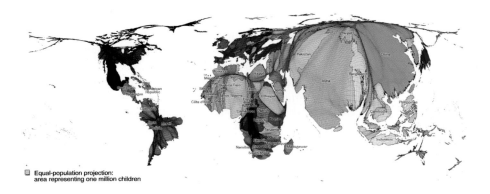

Equal-population projection:
area representing one million children

Figure 10.1 A different view of the world – its children, 2010

Note: Named countries are those included in the surveys reported in this chapter.

Source: SEDAC Columbia University (2010).

of the world. Just under a decade ago a report was published that sought to 'produce the first accurate and reliable measure of the extent and severity of child poverty in the developing world using internationally agreed definitions of poverty' (Gordon, D. et al., 2003, *Child Poverty in the Developing World*, Townsend Centre of International Poverty Research Report for UNICEF, University of Bristol, UK, p. 7). In this chapter some of the data presented in that report is used to map many aspects of poverty around the world.

The UNICEF report used data from demographic and health surveys in 46 countries that contained over half of the world's children to calculate the numbers of children living in poverty in each place. Here the data for all 45 of those countries which each contained more than half a million children are depicted. All the countries of the world are shown coloured separately in Figure 10.1, where the size of each small part of each country is drawn in proportion to the number of children living there. For those countries with survey data it is these areas which are shaded in the remainder of the maps in this chapter. In these surveys, households containing, in total, 1.2 million children were interviewed in the years around the millennium. The figures shown here are largely contemporaneous with the UK's own 2001 census.

From the results of the global surveys, in each of nine maps that follow, these 45 countries are shaded lightest pink if less than one-fifth of children are suffering from the form of poverty being depicted, three medium shades if the proportion suffering is between one-fifth and four-fifths of all children, and dark red if over four-fifths of all children in these countries are so affected. The rest of the world is shaded with hatching because no comparable data were available for the children of those countries. In the affluent countries of the world almost no children will be suffering the forms of poverty detailed in these next nine maps. The final two world maps in this series chart two different measures of the aggregate burden of poverty on the lives of the majority of the children of the world.

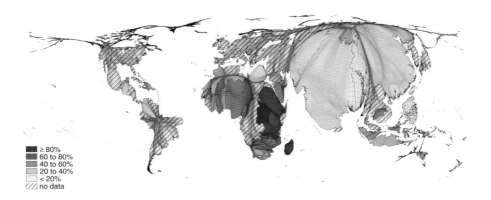

Figure 10.2 Severe water deprivation for children in the world, 2000
Source: UNICEF report.

For children, severe water deprivation is defined as only having access to surface water (i.e. not piped) for drinking, or living in a household where the nearest source of water is more than 15 minutes travel time away. Such children are deprived of water both by quantity and almost certainly through its quality as well. Among the countries plotted in Figure 10.2, over half of all the children living in Rwanda, Uganda, Ethiopia, Madagascar, Tanzania, Kenya, Cambodia, Mozambique, Chad, Cameroon, Malawi, the Central African Republic and Ghana were deprived of water in this way. All of these countries were governed by colonial European powers in the past, including the British.

Over one-fifth of all children in the poor majority of the world only have access to unsafe or distant sources of water, and they are most likely to live in these conditions if their land was once directly governed by the countries in which such deprivation is now unknown. It is the children living outside the towns and cities in these countries who are most likely to suffer such deprivation, although in cities piped supplies can easily be contaminated with sewage through leaks.

The children of the world who are deprived of safe water are, of course, much more likely to die in childhood or young adulthood, but billions will survive for longer. Diseases flourish where water supplies are poor, and human beings are weakened through these deprivations. A century and a half ago cholera epidemics were commonplace in London due to the quality of the water. For those children who survive these deprivations today, a tiny minority will later travel to affluent nations and see for themselves the riches there. The monies required to supply every child in the world with clean water are far less than the amount which the countries of the West spend on their pet food.

It is not a lack of worldwide resources which deprives children of water, but lack of political will to provide it. The children who do not have access to safe water are those children whom people with power do not value at all highly. However, depending on where they live, the children of the poor majority of the world have differing chances of being deprived of different things. The particular

Figure 10.3   Severe sanitation deprivation for children in the world, 2000
Source: UNICEF report.

histories of countries, their physical geography and current economic worth, all influence these patterns.

Figure 10.3 shows where the children most deprived of sanitation live. These are children who have no access to toilet facilities of any kind in (or near to) where they live. For these children there are neither private nor communal toilets nor even pit latrines, nor is there any systematic means of sewage disposal. Over half the children living in Nepal, Ethiopia, Cambodia, Niger, Burkina Faso, Benin, Chad, India, Namibia, Togo, Madagascar, Mozambique, Yemen, Mauritania and Pakistan lack such facilities. As I write, in late spring 2012, more recent comparable surveys of these countries have been conducted, but the data from them has yet to be released. If there have been improvements we will only know from them having been systematically measured and reported.

The largest group of children denied decent basic sanitation live within what were the borders of India, as defined when the British ruled the subcontinent. Ironically, Britain was among the first countries in the world to introduce near-nationwide sewerage and sanitation infrastructure which helped end the cholera outbreaks inside its own shores and turned the tide of many other diseases. In fact, it has been claimed that the introduction of this infrastructure did more to improve the health of the British population than any medical intervention.

To afford such facilities the British required the profits gained by owning India. There is thus a direct link between the sanitation that children in the UK enjoy today, with much of their sewage still flowing through Victorian sewers, and the lack of sanitation seen across India and in other parts of the globe which were once governed from abroad to extract the profits that made the affluent countries rich. Areas like India were not home to such a concentration of the poorest children in the world before colonial rule.

Figure 10.4   Severe shelter deprivation for children in the world, 2000
Source: UNICEF report.

Shelter is the most basic of necessities in the world. Children can travel to find water, can use open ground or distant latrines for sanitation, but without adequate shelter they will physically suffer regardless of their other efforts. Being severely deprived of shelter here is measured as living in a place where there are more than five people per room, or which has mud flooring. Some 34% of the children of these countries live in such circumstances (compared with 31% who are most severely deprived of sanitation). Such accommodation provides near-perfect circumstances to harbour disease, to offer no privacy, and to weaken bodies to ease the spread of infection. Figure 10.4 shows where shelter is most lacking for children amongst these 45 countries.

Because the data on which the figures in this chapter are based was derived from household surveys, they provide no measures of children who are completely homeless. A majority of children in the following countries were severely deprived of adequate shelter: Chad, Ethiopia, Nepal, Bangladesh, Rwanda, Uganda, Niger, Malawi, Tanzania, Central African Republic, Mali, Mauritania, Burkina Faso, Mozambique, Kenya, Namibia, Nicaragua, Zambia, Yemen, Guatemala, Cameroon, Guinea and Peru. The countries in this list (and the other lists in this chapter) are sorted in order from 96% of all children in Chad, to those where the rate is nearer 50%.

Compare Figure 10.4 with the map of people living in homes with seven or more rooms in Britain (Figure 9.7), and try to imagine living with six, seven, eight or more people in one room, or with a floor made of mud. Note also how rates are highest in African countries and in India, and lower in many of those countries usually not governed, at least directly, by colonial powers in the past, such as in South America and parts of East Asia and China. In fact, the lake around which the greatest concentration of children in the world live without adequate shelter, shown on the map in Africa, is named after Queen Victoria. Her name is also used to describe a form of spacious housing ('Victorian' housing) which began to be built in the UK during her reign.

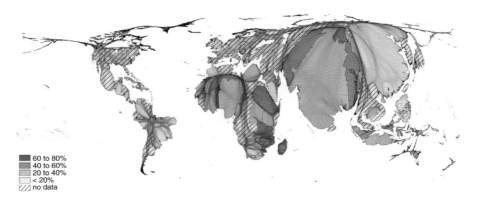

60 to 80%
40 to 60%
20 to 40%
< 20%
no data

Figure 10.5   Severe information deprivation for children in the world, 2000
Source: UNICEF report.

In the poorer countries of the world children are not simply deprived of the physical necessities of life – shelter, water, sanitation and (as we turn to shortly) food. They are also deprived of education, health care and basic information. Children suffering from severe information deprivation are defined as those aged between 3 and 18 who have no access to newspapers, radio or a television where they live. Globally, one-quarter of all children in the poor majority of the world are deprived of basic sources of information.

The children most deprived of information can be seen from Figure 10.5 to clearly be most concentrated in much of Africa and also within the Indian subcontinent. However, information deprivation is also the experience of a majority of children in Benin, Ethiopia and Chad. Elsewhere most children do have access to one of these forms of information, more often than they do to clean water, shelter or sanitation. The very fact that such a high proportion of children do have access to such information illustrates the degree to which information is valued.

A majority of the world's children only achieve very basic literacy. Even in areas of Britain up to almost one-quarter of adults are judged to be functionally illiterate (Figure 6.7). Thus radio and television are the primary means by which information can be transferred, and both these means require a broadcast network and a power grid if even the most basic of radio signals are to be transmitted and received. It is where both education levels are lowest and such infrastructure is least developed that information is most scarce. As information without knowledge is of less value, so it is to education that we turn next.

Figure 10.6 maps the proportions of children in the 45 countries being studied who are severely deprived of education. This is the proportion of children in each country aged between 7 and 18 who have never been to school. They are thus children who have received no formal education of any kind. Partly because the proportion of children in this situation in China is less than 1%, the international proportion is only 13% of all children in these countries. However, this is a very strict definition of educational deprivation. Spend one day in a school

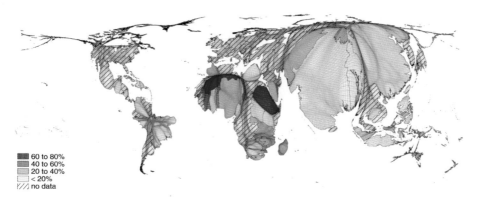

Figure 10.6 Severe educational deprivation for children in the world, 2000
Source: UNICEF report.

in your life and you are no longer deprived by this measure. Over half the children of Niger, Mali, Burkina Faso, Ethiopia, Chad and Guinea are severely educationally deprived even by this strictest of standards.

Girls are far more likely than boys to be educationally deprived, and deprivation is almost everywhere greater in rural areas. Such a pattern would not be out of place in Britain two centuries ago, and puts the current maps in Chapter 3 of this book into stark context. While one of the most telling aspects of the underlying population landscape of the UK is reflected by children's life chances of attending university, the world map of educational disadvantage concerns questions such as whether a single day of the most basic primary education has ever been received. Such a measure hides far greater proportions of children who receive only the most limited education and never learn to read or write at a simple level, and it disguises the impossibility of ever attending a university for the majority of the world's children. However, attending a university is often not even a dream for those who are constantly hungry.

Some 15% of the children of the poor majority of the world are severely deprived of food. The definition of this deprivation is that it includes all children who are so severely malnourished, stunted and emaciated that their heights and weights are more than three standard deviations below the median of the international reference population. Thus the measure includes all children who are most severely wasted, stunted or underweight. To allow for international comparability the proportions reported here are for all children aged less than five years old, but they are representative of older children too.

At the time when the UK 2001 census was asking which households had three or more cars, in no country were as many as half of all children routinely severely food deprived, but in some over one-quarter were. The highest proportions of between one-quarter and one-third of all children being so severely undernourished were found in Bangladesh, Niger, Ethiopia, Nepal, India, Mali and Madagascar. Thus Figure 10.7 only differentiates countries by two shades of

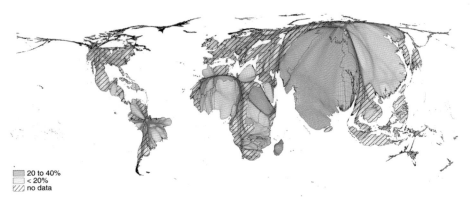

20 to 40%
< 20%
no data

Figure 10.7 Severe food deprivation for children in the world, 2000
Source: UNICEF report.

colour because higher rates of food deprivation do not routinely occur. Rates were lowest in Colombia, the Dominican Republic and Brazil. Although this is a very severe measure of food deprivation, it is useful to consider that the researchers who decided how to grade each form of deprivation used in the UNICEF report concluded, in effect, that lack of access to clean water, sanitation and shelter are more widespread than continued severe lack of access to food.

The stereotype of the children of poor nations starving is misguided. Starvation on a greater scale than this would result in population declines. Note again, however, that it is in many of the places which Britain once governed where the most children go continuously hungry to an extent that their bodies are severely deformed by age five. There is, of course, far more food to be eaten than these children could ever consume, and in the UK many children are consuming far too much. The problem is not its production, but distribution, which is currently carried out according to how these children are valued in monetary terms. Under current world trading rules, thin poor children are not worth feeding as much as fat rich children.

The rarity of widespread fatal starvation is one reason why the population of children in the poorer parts of the world can still rise rapidly. The other major reason is health care and in particular inoculation to prevent disease. For Figure 10.8 a child with severe health deprivation is defined as a child who has not been immunised against any diseases or a young child who has had a recent illness involving diarrhoea and has not received any medical advice or treatment. Diarrhoea is the most common cause of death in infants in the world, although it, and in fact all infectious diseases combined, are such a rare group of cause of death in Britain that they are not separately identified among the causes of death which end Chapter 7 (Table 7.1).

In Britain some (on average more affluent) people actually choose not to have their children immunised, as they have become less concerned about disease and more concerned about extremely unlikely (usually unspecified) side-effects.

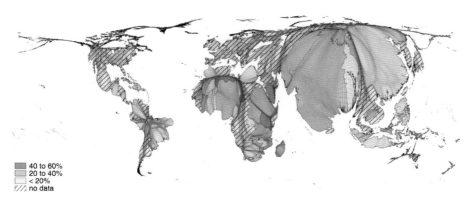

40 to 60%
20 to 40%
< 20%
no data

Figure 10.8 Severe health care deprivation for children in the world, 2000
Source: UNICEF report.

Across the poor majority of the world some 15% of all children are severely deprived of health care, slightly more than are deprived of food. Only in Chad is a majority so deprived and in China less than 1% are. Thus, as for education, the children of China do not feature on this map.

In China the state has the power to ensure that almost all children receive very basic health care and education. Why this is not possible in the world's largest democracy – India – is a crucial question for those who believe that greater freedom of one particular type brings greater prosperity to all. However, due partly to the widespread diffusion of immunisation as a means to prevent disease, and to very basic health advice or treatment being available to 85% of the children in these countries, children's numbers are growing rapidly. It is predicted that this growth will slow to stability within the next generation, but that would require great improvements to the statistics shown here, as poorer families have good reasons to try for more offspring.

Figure 10.9, below, presents a combination of the last seven measures to estimate where overall deprivation is most severe among the 45 countries. Because the data used to measure deprivation came from surveys of households with children it is possible to calculate the proportion of children in each country who suffer from any one of the seven forms of severe deprivation as identified by the UNICEF report. By this measure over 90% of the children of the following countries suffer at least one such deprivation: Nepal, Ethiopia, Chad, Rwanda, Uganda, Burkina Faso, Benin, Bangladesh, Tanzania, Niger, Cambodia, Malawi and Mauritania.

Only in the Philippines, South Africa, the Dominican Republic, Brazil, Colombia and China do more than half of all children escape suffering at least one form of severe deprivation. Thus the majority of children in the poor majority of the world suffer from at least one form of severe deprivation. Rates are highest in Africa and the Indian subcontinent. Because the majority of the world's children live in these or similar areas and because all these measures err towards underestimating deprivation, it is safe to say that half the children in

Figure 10.9 Severe overall deprivation for children in the world, 2000
Source: UNICEF report.

the world by 2000 lacked access to at least one of the following: decent water, sanitation, shelter, information, education, food and health care.

Taken as a whole, as a global population, human beings have never had so much, never consumed so much, never found treating water, building sewers and homes, providing news, schools, food or medicines so easy. The world is awash with the products of our collective labours. However, we have simultaneously managed to distribute these goods so that most children in the world do not have access to at least one of the most basic necessities of a decent life. Few in Britain would tolerate a single child in that country being deprived of any of these necessities and yet we tolerate the majority of children in the world growing up without consistently ensuring them for all but a small minority.

Where, though, do the poorest of the poor live? The causes of children living in severe deprivation are almost always a lack of resources or income. It is possible, however, that some children will suffer deprivation because of some form of discrimination, such as girls not being educated, or will suffer from stunted growth because they contracted a disease, but did not live in the poorest of families. Thus if you are interested in an even more sure measure of deprivation, a measure that the authors of the UNICEF report termed 'absolute' deprivation, then with survey data you can measure the proportion of children suffering from at least two forms of severe deprivation.

The 'absolute' deprivation measure also helps identify where the poorest of poor children live. Over one-third, 37%, of children in all these countries were living in such absolute poverty. Over three-quarters of the children of Ethiopia, Nepal, Chad, Rwanda, Uganda, Niger, Burkina Faso, Tanzania and Mozambique were living in such conditions shortly after the turn of the millennium. The poorest of the poor children of the world are mostly growing up in Africa. They

Figure 10.10   Absolute overall deprivation for children in the world, 2000
Source: UNICEF report.

live just a few thousand miles to the South of us, in a continent which the UK's 14 million children would fit into 33 times.

For every child in the UK there are thus 33 children in Africa, most growing up in absolute poverty and almost all being severely deprived of at least one of the basic human needs. The surveys on which these figures were based involved interviewing the households of about one child in every 650 in Africa. This is a remarkable feat. Surveying in some of the poorest countries, such as Somalia, was not possible. Since the surveys were taken conditions in some countries like Somalia are known to have worsened, and food price speculation by financiers has resulted in price hikes and more starvation than usual, especially among children. It is thus unlikely that numbers shown here overestimate the extent and depth of poverty on the African continent. However, elsewhere the conditions will have improved. To be sure of where and by how much always requires more censuses and surveys.

AN EXERCISE

Mapping the population of the world is far more difficult than charting it within one rich nation for which there is abundant information. National censuses are often not taken in many countries, so the results of surveys can be hard to compare. Most importantly of all, international statistics are almost always presented for states which vary enormously in population and for which averages tend to disguise huge internal variations.

The surveys that were used to generate the figures used to shade the maps in this chapter did differentiate almost universally between children living in rural or urban settlements, and that alone showed that the worst conditions were concentrated out of the cities. Why else would so many people in poor countries be leaving the land for the cities?

One day soon maps will be drawn of the entire world's population that will differentiate both within countries as well as between them. The map base used here is the very first that could do this, but only if we had data for within country distributions as well as between country variations. Such maps will depict an even more starkly divided world than that shown in these pages on which, after all, the maps only depict up to 45 statistics. Suppose we had information on every square of the world cartogram, on the living conditions of every geographical concentration of 1 million children in the world. The maps would still be presenting averages of huge numbers of people, but for 2,150 regions rather than just 45 countries. How might such a map look?

To begin, draw an example of how a new world map might appear for the 14 million children of the UK. First, you need to draw your base map. You could use the outline drawn in the world maps in this book, or a simpler one in which the Kingdom is allocated 14 squares on the map in a shape which very roughly approximates its boundaries. A rough example is provided in Figure 10.11 where the regions and countries of the Kingdom have each been allocated a square, the South East and Scotland, both with the largest numbers of children, being allocated two squares. You need not use this example. Instead you could combine groups of six or seven of the European constituencies used in this book. One year's worth of their children are counted in Figure 1.3 (see underlying data).

Next, each choose one example from this book of a variable for your 14 areas. Remember that as each of the areas used in this book contain roughly equal

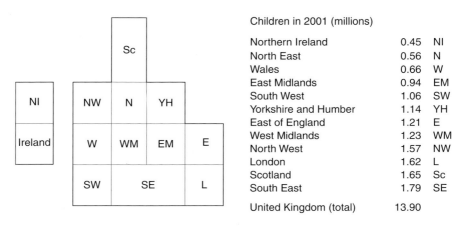

Children in 2001 (millions)

Northern Ireland	0.45	NI
North East	0.56	N
Wales	0.66	W
East Midlands	0.94	EM
South West	1.06	SW
Yorkshire and Humber	1.14	YH
East of England	1.21	E
West Midlands	1.23	WM
North West	1.57	NW
London	1.62	L
Scotland	1.65	Sc
South East	1.79	SE
United Kingdom (total)	13.90	

Figure 10.11   Example: regional cartogram of the children of the UK

Note: The UK represented by 14 squares.

Source: 2001 Census data.

populations, in most cases you can simply sum proportions shown on these maps and divide them by the number of areas you are considering to calculate an average proportion for, which is representative of that group as a whole. Having drawn your map, next compare it to the original map of variation over 84 or 85 areas. How much of the original detail do you lose? The answer to that question depends on how much variation within regions there was to begin with.

A good example to take in the context of this chapter is employment in the financial industries, as depicted in Figure 8.2. You will have to look at the website for this book to find the underlying data (see link on this page: www.dannydorling.org).

To calculate the 2001 proportion in, say, London, simply sum all the proportions in the London areas shown in that website (both the 1991 and the change proportions) and divide the result by 10, as there are ten areas in London.

It should not take you too long to draw one map of what could be part of a future depiction of the human geography of the whole world's workforce in financial industries.

Compare the maps that you have drawn and answer the following questions:

1 Which design appears to work best, is most visually appealing and presents the data both as simply and as accurately as appears possible?

2 Which design could most easily be extended to draw out a map of all the areas in the world in which 1 million children live?

3 How should such a world map be drawn, on where should it be centred, how should it be oriented (what should be at the top)?

4 To what extent does the loss of detail matter when this image is just part of a much larger picture? Does it really matter precisely which areas you combine to group a million children?

5 What information, if any, could you find to draw out variations in the globe in this way? Why is that information in some areas so limited, and will there continue to be countries for the foreseeable future which will simply be labelled 'no data'?

6 What is the point of mapping the geography of people's lives in more detail? Does it serve a useful purpose or simply reinforce what we think we already know of our humanity and inhumanity?

Conclusion

In looking abroad we can begin to see the context within which the human geography of the UK is placed. There is very little which is tangible about the borders of this Kingdom and I have been liberal throughout these pages in variously referring to that entity, or Britain, or occasionally omitting Scotland, and at no point have I yet explained how or why the British are actually citizens of a European Union that now spans most of that continent, nor that their major industries and corporations are often as at home in New York as in London.

A chapter on the world context to the human geography of the UK could have discussed international forces, the now rapid movements of monies around the globe, international travel, the spread of the English language, the ever present fear and reality of world recession/depression or of future world wars of whatever kind. However, such an approach would have ignored the majority of the people of the world and in studying population it is still the human context which matters most. Who are all those people around you?

People are easily forgotten if you chart, map and describe the non-human worlds which influence our lives, the worlds of power, exploitation, profit and fear. All these worlds are created by people, but to see the context within which we are placed simply in these terms reduces the majority of the world's people, and especially the world's children to the sidelines. Fundamentally, the human geography of the world that best describes its population is a map made up of people and how they are distributed across the planet, how they will be distributed in the future, how they are living today and what their millions of hopes, fears, needs and aspirations are, which is the context that most matters to the British population of one small island; an island which in the past had a huge influence on most of the peoples of the rest of the world, a past which is reflected in the human geography of that island, and a past which almost certainly will matter more in the future.

Almost half the world was once governed directly or indirectly from ministries in London. Most of those colonies are now free but London's clerks, soldiers and civil servants have been replaced by an even greater army of financiers, bankers, insurers and underwriters. Along with New York (and to a far lesser extent Tokyo), London still exerts a hugely undue influence on the world in proportion to its population. Furthermore, that influence is not planned, not thought out; it is the product of billions of financial transactions a year. Each transaction is a decision which at the time appears rational, or at least seems a good guess, concerning moving money or risk around in a way that is hopefully profitable at that moment in time.

When the first edition of this book was written, in 2005, in aggregate and on average, almost all the financial transactions being made in London were extremely profitable for the people who were making them, and there was increasingly little else underwriting the economy of the Kingdom. This increased profitability of finance was the key driving force that was altering the human geography of Britain;

it is why the young and able were moving South in such numbers, and why lives to the North and West looked more and more different. Within the UK it was the uneven distribution of the spoils of such financial gain which was the most important driver of growing social inequalities. Even after the great banking crash of 2008 it is again those gains which are seen as the major hope for the future.

It matters where the profit is made. However, it matters also where it comes from. Money cannot be made out of thin air. Why do the bankers of the world come to London to raise their loans? Why does London still house some of the insurers of last resort? What do we have which is so needed by the rest of the world that they pay us tithes, in effect, for our advice, time and acumen? After all, money is easily moved. Why have the world's bankers not moved to Mumbai, Rio or Hong Kong? London is often a cold, wet and dreary place to live, its empire long gone, its countryside stripped of its most easily extracted resources and most of its people not living in a state of luxury. In the capital itself is found one of the largest concentrations of poverty in any rich nation in the world. Britain is no longer a military power of much substance, and most of its infrastructure, its buildings, sewers, railways and roads are old. Why here and why now?

A large part of the reason for the UK's continued success as a world banker is inertia. However, inertia cannot explain why that success was growing until 2008, why more and more of the world's money was flowing through London and why more and more people were employed there to help take a slice off it as it travelled through. Of course most of the financial service workers of London do not work in international finance. They help cycle monies within the Kingdom in the form of pensions, insurance and loans, but these activities alone cannot generate extra money. It is the much smaller numbers of people who invest the pension funds, underwrite the insurance firms and raise the capital from outside the Kingdom to make millions of loans possible who actually bring money into the UK.

Increasingly, people with money in the rest of the world trusted people in London to look after their money for them. They felt safer dealing with the largest of banks and companies, those which had offices in every major city and their headquarters in England or America. This even applied to banks found, by the summer of 2012, to have been illegally manipulating interest rates. Why were they so trusted? What had happened over time to bolster that trust, to end up with companies and governments thousands of miles away increasingly doing business in a European capital which they knew would extract a profit from them? Turn to look at the state of most of the children of the world as just one possible reason.

The majority of the children of the world live in a state of severe poverty, more than one-third live in absolute deprivation. In the countries where most of these children live, and in the regions around them, what does the future look like? How safe are the governments of these countries? How likely is revolution and/or war? How secure are their financial institutions? How safe are their peoples from disease, famine, crime and disorder? Then look again at the maps of world poverty among children in this chapter. In terms of people, where is the nation-state that is situated furthest from the poor majority who will be the adults of this century? Which country is furthest from areas coloured various shades on these maps?

Which country sits in the only ocean of the world, the North Atlantic, not to be bordered by coastlines where children lack water, sanitation, basic education, health care, food, information and shelter? Where would you put your money, do your deals, if you wanted both it and them to be safe in the future? London does not have a unique advantage in geographical isolation. There are many places around the world where finance is booming, often in very small islands less regulated by government control and where faster profits can be made. Often, though, it turns out that these 'Treasure Islands' are underwritten themselves by London banking. London benefits both from its past and its current position. Money comes to London because it flows away from where most people need it and from where one day they might try to take it back.

Further Reading

It is about time I actually recommended another book rather than just more and more websites to read. Luckily, however, many books now have their own website. One great one is the website of the book *Treasure Islands* by Nicholas Shazson (http://treasureislands.org/), which contains up-to-the-minute news about how the rich are getting richer at the expense of the poor worldwide. This is a tragedy, but what is even sadder is that the rich are not necessarily really benefitting from their gains. See the website of Oliver James' book *Affluenza* to read more on that (www.selfishcapitalist.com/affluenza.html), especially the section on his other books. Last, in case you are thinking that maybe there are just too many people in the world and it might be inevitable that other people's children are going hungry, that there are just too many of us to feed, then get your thinking sorted out by getting hold of a copy of Ian Angus and Simon Butler's book *Too Many People*. All the details can be found at www.haymarketbooks. org/pb/Too-Many-People .... So, what are you waiting for?

Key Point Summary

- The majority of children in the word still lack what in Britain is usually taken for granted.

- The economic success of the UK is partly reliant on other places being insecure.

- The majority of the world's children are poor partly because of actions of people in Britain.

11

FUTURE

... concluding the Kingdom

The UK is made up of many small islands dominated by one small island: Britain. Less than 1% of the world's population lives in the UK. Most of these people were born in just a few hundred maternity units and attended one or two of a few thousand secondary schools. If trends in 2010 had continued then within just a few years a majority would have gone to university, most of them to just a few dozen campuses.

One-third of the population lives in the few largest conurbations. By the area names and boundaries used in this book (and given their European constituency areas on these pages in brackets), these conurbations are quick to list and the first is almost as large as the rest: London (10), Greater Manchester (3), Birmingham (2), Merseyside (2), Bristol (1), Glasgow (1), Leeds (1), Leicester (1), Sheffield (1) and Tyne & Wear (1).

There is great interest within some geography circles in the Kingdom as to which city and conurbation holds what rank in any urban order – where their precise boundaries end and so on. However, a list as crude as that just given is as good as any. What matters is that the Kingdom is simply a small place. The domination by one conurbation is far more important than the scrabbling around of others to vie to be recognised as being in second, third, or even tenth place.

Most people in the UK live within 100 miles of half the population of the main island. This has been the case for many decades and, although the human geography of the UK is slowly changing, what characterises it as most unusual, internationally, is how slow that change has been for most of the last 100 years.

Many places in the UK are still populated because they were populated in the distant past and homes were built there. Other land is relatively sparsely populated. In the South of England this is usually because it was sparsely populated in the past and that past is being preserved (rather than a lack of demand to live there). To the North and West large amounts of land are designated National Parks specifically to fossilise the visual appearance of their human-created landscapes. And it is not just here that time appears to be passing slowly.

Outside the countryside most cities, towns, suburbs and even streets which were rich or poor a century ago are in much the same relative position now. Relatively stable population growth and then stagnation, along with strict planning controls and, most importantly, a remarkable degree of snobbishness (among those who can choose where to live), and a sense that place and location matter, have helped to ensure that they do, and do so more now than place has mattered for many decades.

The majority of variation across the human landscape of the UK can be revealed by dividing that landscape up into just the seven dozen areas used in this book and treating Northern Ireland as an additional slightly bigger area, just as those who designed the original European parliamentary constituencies chose to do. The Province was mainly described with the words 'no data' in the first edition of this book and, although unfortunate from the point of view of people interested in its human geography, that perhaps best still describes it in terms of both how it is viewed from Britain and how the British state tends to exclude it from its national datasets.

It was a bit cheeky to claim that this book is about the population of the UK given how little data on the Province it originally included, unless you sign up to the argument that this is how the Province is mostly represented within the UK: as not being there. In this edition most of the gaps have been filled in and data for Northern Ireland is now usually included. Often it was released later than for much of the rest of UK and so could not be included before.

Turning to the mainland, the remaining 84 areas for which we mostly do have comparable data are a relatively arbitrary subdivision of Britain. The subdivision is unique as a regional description of these countries only in that, unlike any other, it divides the population up into equally sized groups. That has great advantages in revealing the main contours of the landscape. Similarly, the presentation of variation of these areas as a visual landscape is also novel.

Most depictions of the human geography of the UK concentrate on just 12 or so regions and countries. The standard regions (or Government Office Regions) are areas which deliberately mix up town and country and rich and poor, and thus hide the majority of the variation in the landscape. Over the last couple of decades a dozen atlases of the human geography of parts of the UK have been drawn at finer spatial scales, but most of the variation they show is also revealed in these pages. It is between these 85 areas that the lines that are most crucial to dividing up the population of the UK roughly lie.

The patterns to life in the UK do become more detailed, more fascinating and increasingly more revealing as smaller and smaller groups of people are mapped, but such pictures are merely elaborations on the basic spatial social divisions revealed here. Within each European constituency another 85 or so areas could be drawn, showing, in most, variation akin to that found nationally but with divides that were less stark. That exercise could be repeated again, resulting in some 600,000 areas each containing roughly 85 adults.

Only at a very fine level of detail would we begin to see a different nature to the human landscape emerge. Individual enclosures of extreme affluence and poverty would become clear, but most of the areas would appear more uniform. If you take two short streets in the UK at random, each containing about 85 people, they are unlikely to differ very much in their social characteristics. It is not until you group people in very large numbers by where they live that, for most, you begin to see the importance of place everywhere.

Accounts of the human geography of the UK, just like this one, tend to concentrate on what most differentiates people, the peaks and troughs of the landscape, its steepest slopes, cliffs and other disjunctures. However, a great deal of the landscape is, in detail, quite uniform even if, over time, it has been becoming a little less so. Even on the simple maps in this book your eye is naturally drawn to try to see what is most interesting and to ignore the ways in which most places are nearly average. However, this underlying uniformity, the slight social differences revealed within it and the sharp divides that consistently separate a few places from the rest all require the same careful and continuous maintenance for this landscape to be preserved as it is.

People in the UK, over a long period of time, have to behave and be controlled in very consistent ways to keep the suburbs nondescript, the inner cities mostly poor, the Home Counties mostly affluent and the periphery peripheral. Historically, children must act much like their parent(s) did before them. Socially, people must behave like their peers. Economically, cohorts must act lemming-like in reacting to what collectively hits them due to the timing of their births. Politically, people must act a little more like their neighbours than they otherwise might if our maps of the landscape are to continue to look neat.

Were future generations to behave very differently from their elders as they age, were people's actions not largely predictable from those of their social peers, were cohorts not to accept their historical fate and neighbours their spatial obligations to act similarly to one another, it would become harder and harder to describe the population landscape of the UK. To extend the physical metaphor, it would be like water beginning to flow uphill, mountains coming crashing down, smooth slopes becoming pitted and unchartable.

Fortunately, if only for the cartographers of this particular landscape, the British population do not go in for revolution, their governments occasionally try more enthusiastically than usual to prop up areas which are faring poorly and curtail the extravagances in places where affluence amasses, but, in the main, we (in our actions) and they (in their Acts) function as gardeners maintaining the look of a landscape largely created in Victorian times. Sometimes more callous politicians try to take the landscape back a little more towards those times.

Largely despite those who rule us, we tend to produce roughly the right numbers of babies and attract in-migrants to fill the homes of the future, largely bring our children up where and how we are supposed to, fill almost all of the school and university places allocated to us, take the entry-level jobs on offer, buy homes when we can as soon as we can afford to, retire or drop out as ill when we are told or feel we are no longer needed, and finally move compliantly in our dotages away from places where the young are most needed. Those of us with money leave much of it to our families so they can afford to buy where we once lived. Were any of these patterns to change, much of the landscape would quickly erode and reform.

Internal to the UK there are a few trends which could be highlighted for those interested in how the future geography of the UK might differ. Until very recently fewer children were being born per woman than at any time in the last century, and being born later in most women's lives. Half of all young women in England now go to university. More women than men are now receiving the 'best' qualifications and many more young men have left the UK than we realised before we took the 2001 census. The 2011 census will tell us much more.

Many more children are being educated to higher levels than ever before, although still in such a way that they are socially sorted much as their parents were. Today's children (and now young adults) are simply tested far more, given more certificates and, until recently, made to wait a few more years before being allowed entry into the workforce. However, recently even delayed entry has begun to look uncertain for growing numbers. Very many doubt they will get a steady job, or ever be able to take out a mortgage, let alone pay it off. Far too few still ask who would be getting rich by lending them the money.

Even if the current economic crisis recedes there are other changes likely to make the lives of the next generation very different from their parents'. Those of the next generation who manage to find work are entering a workforce now more divided geographically, socially and economically than that in which their parent(s) laboured. More jobs are now either menial or labelled as 'professional' than in the past and remunerated more unequally accordingly.

The enhanced division of labour is being reflected in the landscape as the price of entry into many places diverges, as reflected through house prices. It is reflected in new layers in the sediment beneath the surface as the patterns to our mortality become ever more geographically distinct. And, as more people die than are being born, higher numbers are being allowed to emigrate to the UK from abroad, and so another future change that could be highlighted is in people's more disparate geographical origins. But the UK has, when it has suited it, allowed and encouraged similar proportions in from abroad before.

If anything, it is external influences on the UK that are most likely to alter the landscape in the future and which, it could be argued, did most to determine its shape in the past and present. The South is richer basically because of where it is and hence where it was and is nearer to. It remains rich because of the hold of more people there over the levers of power, but they held those levers partly because of their position in a more widely drawn world.

Place the UK in the Mediterranean sea and the capital would lie near the mountainous north. The ten cities listed at the start of this conclusion grew up on the profits of organising empire, and on cotton, shipping, wool, steel, coal and iron – their export, import and commodification. The great depressions and greatest recession of the last century, separated by 50 years, were worldwide events, the impacts of which are still etched in the human landscape of the UK. The first great recession/depression of this century came about just 30 years later. Is economic instability accelerating?

Just as booms and busts have long-lasting effects, the legacies of two world wars are still felt in numerous ways, most obviously as the survivors of the million babies born in celebration in 1946 turned 65 in 2011. Finding out what has happened to commuter-belt suburbs when such a large group no longer needs to live there will be interesting, especially as the young are choosing or being forced to live for longer in city centres – another global trend.

The demand for the labour and skills of the young in these cities is increasingly financed internationally too. We consume far more than we physically produce and can only do so because of the financial services we sell abroad. Were international trust in the UK – and in London in particular – to fall, the result would, in the short term at least, be devastating. Only just over half a percentage of the world's children live in the UK as compared to its whole percentage of the world's adults, and thus the Kingdom is set to halve in size on the global map of our human landscape. Much more is both going on and changing outside, as compared to within.

Although the UK is a tiny speck on the global landscape, and is set to become smaller still, it holds a position of disproportionate importance on that world map. This is not just through its impact in consuming far more than it produces, in its influence on far-away nations through world markets, through its continued military adventures or its luck in being home to the language of international trade and the Internet. The UK is also disproportionately important in being the setting for one of the longest-running social experiments in the world.

What happens when you allow people to elect their masters over a long period of time, when your policies to shape the landscape have not been interrupted by invasion or revolution, when your population has been largely stable in location, when your wealth has been great, when you have lived through generation after generation of social reform, when you have paid pensions for almost a century, provided free health care for over half a century, when you have had most of the advantages of location (worldwide) for longer than almost anywhere else and have had an empire to help pay for your projects until recently?

What occurs in these 'almost the best of circumstances' that Britain, until 2008, enjoyed is an experiment in tempering capitalism. Our landscape reveals how a population organised through markets and moderated by its government behaves. This is how people become sorted out over space if you organise life in such a way. What we can see now and should expect in the future is perhaps the best that we can expect to get – if this is how we collectively choose to behave.

Where the British behave worse is, perhaps, in tolerating levels of inequality far higher than are found acceptable in almost all other affluent nations. However, in early July 2012 one of the UK's highest paid bankers, Bob Diamond, was forced to resign over accusations of impropriety at Barclays, one of the UK's largest banks. It may just have been a glimpse of what is possible, a flash-in-the-pan, or it may have been an early sign of more changes to come, as what was deemed acceptable before becomes no longer tolerable.

Currently economic and social inequalities the UK are not just high but rising rapidly. At times the effects of this are awful, at other times it's not bad, it's not great, it's not fair, it's no utopia, but for most, unless they look ahead a little too keenly (and worry about the climate warming), it is still, just, a pleasant enough brick, concrete and asphalt land; it is planned, maintained, in places agonised over and preserved. It's a very British landscape, a southern English garden with rough edges, sitting in a far less clearly ordered world, the disorder of which it is disproportionately responsible for, and which may matter most for its future in the years to come.

Appendix

The places mapped in this book

This appendix defines each European constituency used in this book in terms of the (approximate) local authority areas which it includes, and the Westminster constituencies included within each, also approximately, as their boundaries existed around 2010. The European constituencies were defined as exact amalgamation of 1997 Westminster Constituencies. That list is given in the appendix to the *Human Geography of the UK* (2005), the first edition of this book.

Area #	European Constituency	2001 Local Authorities	2010 Westminster Constituencies
		London	
1	London Central	Camden LB; City of London; Hammersmith and Fulham LB; Islington LB; Kensington and Chelsea LB; Westminster LB.	Chelsea & Fulham; Cities of London & Westminster; Hammersmith; Hampstead & Kilburn; Holborn & St Pancras; Islington North; Islington South & Finsbury; Kensington; Westminster North
2	London East	Barking and Dagenham LB; Havering LB; Redbridge LB.	Barking; Dagenham & Rainham; East Ham; Hornchurch & Upminster; Ilford North; Ilford South; Romford
3	London North	Barnet LB; Enfield LB; Haringey LB.	Chipping Barnet; Edmonton; Enfield North; Enfield Southgate; Finchley & Golders Green; Hendon; Hornsey & Wood Green; Tottenham
4	London North East	Hackney LB; Newham LB; Tower Hamlets LB; Waltham Forest LB.	Bethnal Green & Bow; Chingford & Woodford Green; Hackney North & Stoke Newington; Hackney South & Shoreditch; Leyton & Wanstead; Poplar & Limehouse; Walthamstow; West Ham
5	London North West	Brent LB; Harrow LB; Hillingdon LB.	Brent Central; Brent North; Harrow East; Harrow West; Hayes & Harlington; Ruislip, Northwood & Pinner; Uxbridge & Ruislip South

(Continued)

(Continued)

Area #	European Constituency	2001 Local Authorities	2010 Westminster Constituencies
6	London South & Surrey East	Croydon LB; Epsom and Ewell LA; Sutton LB; Tandridge LA.	Carshalton & Wallington; Croydon Central; Croydon North; Croydon South; Surrey East; Epsom & Ewell; Sutton & Cheam
7	London South East	Bexley LB; Bromley LB; Greenwich LB.	Beckenham; Bexleyheath & Crayford; Bromley & Chislehurst; Eltham; Erith & Thamesmead; Greenwich & Woolwich; Old Bexley & Sidcup; Orpington
8	London South Inner	Lambeth LB; Lewisham LB; Southwark LB.	Bermondsey & Old Southwark; Camberwell & Peckham; Dulwich & West Norwood; Lewisham East; Lewisham West & Penge; Lewisham Deptford; Streatham; Vauxhall
9	London South West	Kingston upon Thames LB; Merton LB; Wandsworth LB.	Battersea; Kingston & Surbiton; Mitcham & Morden; Putney; Richmond Park; Tooting; Wimbledon
10	London West	Ealing LB; Hounslow LB; Richmond upon Thames LB; Spelthorne LA.	Brentford & Isleworth; Ealing Central & Acton; Ealing North; Ealing Southall; Feltham & Heston; Spelthorne; Twickenham
South East			
11	Buckinghamshire & Oxfordshire East	Aylesbury Vale LA; Cherwell LA; Chiltern LA; South Bucks LA; South Oxfordshire LA; Wycombe LA.	Aylesbury; Banbury; Beaconsfield; Buckingham; Chesham & Amersham; Henley; Wycombe
12	East Sussex & Kent South	Brighton and Hove UA; Eastbourne LA; Hastings LA; Lewes LA; Rother LA; Tunbridge Wells LA; Wealden LA.	Bexhill & Battle; Brighton Kemptown; Brighton Pavilion; Eastbourne; Hastings & Rye; Lewes; Tunbridge Wells; Wealden
13	Hampshire North & Oxford	Basingstoke and Deane LA; Oxford LA; Vale of White Horse LA; West Berkshire UA; West Oxfordshire LA.	Basingstoke; Newbury; Hampshire North West; Oxford East; Oxford West & Abingdon; Wantage; Witney
14	Kent East	Ashford LA; Canterbury LA; Dover LA; Shepway LA; Swale LA; Thanet LA.	Ashford; Canterbury; Dover; Faversham & Kent Mid; Folkestone & Hythe; Thanet North; Sittingbourne & Sheppey; Thanet South

Area #	European Constituency	2001 Local Authorities	2010 Westminster Constituencies
15	Kent West	Dartford LA; Gravesham LA; Maidstone LA; Medway UA; Sevenoaks LA; Tonbridge and Malling LA.	Chatham & Aylesford; Dartford; Gillingham & Rainham; Gravesham; Maidstone & The Weald; Rochester & Strood; Sevenoaks; Tonbridge & Malling
16	South Downs West	Arun LA; Chichester LA; East Hampshire LA; Hart LA; Rushmoor LA; Waverley LA; Winchester LA.	Aldershot; Bognor Regis & Littlehampton; Chichester; Hampshire East; Hampshire North East; Surrey South West; Winchester
17	Surrey	Elmbridge LA; Guildford LA; Mole Valley LA; Reigate and Barnstead LA; Runnymede LA; Surrey Heath LA; Woking LA.	Esher & Walton; Guildford; Mole Valley; Reigate; Runnymede & Weybridge; Surrey Heath; Woking
18	Sussex West	Adur LA; Crawley LA; Horsham LA; Mid Sussex LA; Worthing LA.	Arundel & South Downs; Crawley; Worthing East & Shoreham; Horsham; Hove; Sussex Mid; Worthing West
19	Thames Valley	Bracknell Forest UA; Reading UA; Slough UA; Windsor and Maidenhead UA; Wokingham UA.	Bracknell; Maidenhead; Reading East; Reading West; Slough; Windsor; Wokingham
20	Wight & Hampshire South	Eastleigh LA; Fareham LA; Gosport LA; Havant LA; Isle of Wight UA; Portsmouth UA.	Eastleigh; Fareham; Gosport; Havant; Isle of Wight; Meon Valley; Portsmouth North; Portsmouth South
South West			
21	Bristol	Bristol, City of UA; South Gloucestershire UA.	Bristol East; Bristol North West; Bristol South; Bristol West; Filton & Bradley Stoke; Kingswood; Somerset North; Thornbury & Yate
22	Cornwall & West Plymouth	Caradon LA; Carrick LA; Isles of Scilly LA; Kerrier LA; North Cornwall LA; Penwith LA; Plymouth UA; Restormel LA.	Camborne & Redruth; Cornwall North; Plymouth Moor View; Plymouth Sutton & Devonport; Cornwall South East; St Austell & Newquay; St Ives; Truro & Falmouth

(Continued)

(Continued)

Area #	European Constituency	2001 Local Authorities	2010 Westminster Constituencies
23	Devon & East Plymouth	Exeter LA; Mid Devon LA; South Hams LA; Teignbridge LA; Torbay UA; Torridge LA; West Devon LA.	Devon Central; Devon East; Exeter; Newton Abbot; Devon South West; Tiverton & Honiton; Torbay; Devon West & Torridge; Totnes
24	Dorset & East Devon	Bournemouth UA; East Devon LA; East Dorset LA; North Dorset LA; Poole UA; Purbeck LA; West Dorset LA; Weymouth and Portland LA.	Bournemouth East; Bournemouth West; Dorset Mid & Poole North; Dorset North; Poole; Dorset South; Dorset West
25	Gloucestershire	Cheltenham LA; Cotswold LA; Forest of Dean LA; Gloucester LA; Malvern Hills LA; Stroud LA; Tewkesbury LA.	Cheltenham; Forest of Dean; Gloucester; Stroud; Tewkesbury; Cotswolds, The; Worcestershire West
26	Itchen, Test & Avon	Christchurch LA; New Forest LA; Salisbury LA; Southampton UA; Test Valley LA.	Christchurch; New Forest East; New Forest West; Romsey & Southampton North; Salisbury; Wiltshire South West; Southampton Itchen; Southampton Test
27	Somerset & North Devon	Mendip LA; North Devon LA; North Somerset UA; Sedgemoor LA; South Somerset LA; Taunton Deane LA; West Somerset LA.	Bridgwater & Somerset West; Devon North; Somerton & Frome; Taunton Deane; Wells; Weston-Super-Mare; Yeovil
28	Wiltshire North & Bath	Bath and North East Somerset UA; Kennet LA; North Wiltshire LA; Swindon UA; West Wiltshire LA.	Bath; Chippenham; Devizes; Somerset North East; Swindon North; Wiltshire North; Swindon South
East of England			
29	Bedfordshire & Milton Keynes	Bedford LA; Luton UA; Mid Bedfordshire LA; Milton Keynes UA; South Bedfordshire LA.	Bedford; Luton North; Luton South; Bedfordshire Mid; Milton Keynes North; Milton Keynes South; Bedfordshire North East; Bedfordshire South West

Area #	European Constituency	2001 Local Authorities	2010 Westminster Constituencies
30	Cambridgeshire	Cambridge LA; East Cambridgeshire LA; Fenland LA; Huntingdonshire LA; Peterborough UA; South Cambridgeshire LA.	Cambridge; Huntingdon; Cambridgeshire North East; Cambridgeshire North West; Peterborough; Cambridgeshire South; Cambridgeshire South East
31	Essex North & Suffolk South	Babergh LA; Braintree LA; Chelmsford LA; Colchester LA; Maldon LA; Tendring LA.	Braintree; Chelmsford; Clacton; Colchester; Harwich & Essex North; Maldon; Suffolk South; Witham
32	Essex South	Basildon LA; Castle Point LA; Rochford LA; Southend-on-Sea UA; Thurrock UA.	Basildon & Billericay; Castle Point; Rayleigh & Wickford; Rochford & Southend East; Basildon South & Thurrock East; Southend West; Thurrock
33	Essex West & Hertfordshire East	Brentwood LA; Broxbourne LA; East Hertfordshire LA; Epping Forest LA; Harlow LA; North Hertfordshire LA; Stevenage LA; Uttlesford LA.	Brentwood & Ongar; Broxbourne; Epping Forest; Harlow; Hertford & Stortford; Hertfordshire North East; Saffron Walden; Stevenage
34	Hertfordshire	Dacorum LA; Hertsmere LA; St. Albans LA; Three Rivers LA; Watford LA; Welwyn Hatfield LA.	Hemel Hempstead; Hertsmere; Hitchin & Harpenden; Hertfordshire South West; St Albans; Watford; Welwyn Hatfield
35	Norfolk	Broadland LA; Great Yarmouth LA; King's Lynn and West Norfolk LA; North Norfolk LA; Norwich LA; South Norfolk LA.	Broadland; Great Yarmouth; Norfolk Mid; Norfolk North; Norfolk North West; Norwich North; Norwich South; Norfolk South
36	Suffolk & South West Norfolk	Breckland LA; Forest Heath LA; Ipswich LA; Mid Suffolk LA; St. Edmundsbury LA; Suffolk Coastal LA; Waveney LA.	Bury St Edmunds; Suffolk Central & Ipswich North; Ipswich; Norfolk South West; Suffolk Coastal; Waveney; Suffolk West

(Continued)

(Continued)

Area #	European Constituency	2001 Local Authorities	2010 Westminster Constituencies
West Midlands			
37	Birmingham East	Birmingham MB.	Birmingham Edgbaston; Birmingham Hall Green; Birmingham Hodge Hill; Birmingham Ladywood; Birmingham Northfield; Birmingham Selly Oak; Birmingham Yardley
38	Birmingham West	Sandwell MB; Walsall MB.	Aldridge-Brownhills; Birmingham Erdington; Birmingham Perry Barr; Sutton Coldfield; Walsall North; Walsall South; West Bromwich East; West Bromwich West
39	Coventry & North Warwickshire	Coventry MB; North Warwickshire LA; Nuneaton and Bedworth LA; Solihull MB.	Coventry North East; Coventry North West; Coventry South; Meriden; Warwickshire North; Nuneaton; Rugby; Solihull
40	Herefordshire & Shropshire	Bridgnorth LA; Herefordshire, County of UA; North Shropshire LA; Oswestry LA; Shrewsbury and Atcham LA; South Shropshire LA; Telford and Wrekin UA; Wyre Forest LA.	Hereford & Herefordshire South; Ludlow; Herefordshire North; Shropshire North; Shrewsbury & Atcham; Telford; Wrekin, The; Wyre Forest
41	Midlands West	Dudley MB; Wolverhampton MB.	Dudley North; Dudley South; Halesowen & Rowley Regis; Stourbridge; Warley; Wolverhampton North East; Wolverhampton South East; Wolverhampton South West
42	Staffordshire East & Derby	Cannock Chase LA; Derby UA; East Staffordshire LA; Lichfield LA; South Derbyshire LA; Tamworth LA.	Burton; Cannock Chase; Derby North; Derby South; Lichfield; Derbyshire South; Tamworth
43	Staffordshire West & Congleton	Congleton LA; Newcasle-under-Lyme LA; South Staffordshire LA; Stafford LA; Stoke-on-Trent UA.	Congleton; Newcastle-under-Lyme; Staffordshire South; Stafford; Stoke-on-Trent Central; Stoke-on-Trent North; Stoke-on-Trent South; Stone

Area #	European Constituency	2001 Local Authorities	2010 Westminster Constituencies
44	Worcestershire & South Warwickshire	Bromsgrove LA; Redditch LA; Rugby LA; Stratford-upon-Avon LA; Warwick LA; Worcester LA; Wychavon LA.	Bromsgrove; Kenilworth & Southam; Worcestershire Mid; Redditch; Stratford-on-Avon; Warwick & Leamington; Worcester
East Midlands			
45	Leicester	Harborough LA; Leicester UA; Melton LA; Oadby and Wigston LA; Rutland UA; South Kesteven LA.	Charnwood; Grantham & Stamford; Harborough; Leicester East; Leicester South; Leicester West; Rutland & Melton
46	Lincolnshire	Boston LA; East Lindsey LA; Lincoln LA; North East Lincolnshire UA; North Kesteven LA; South Holland LA; West Lindsey LA.	Boston & Skegness; Cleethorpes; Gainsborough; Great Grimsby; Lincoln; Louth & Horncastle; Sleaford & North Hykeham; South Holland & The Deepings
47	Northamptonshire & Blaby	Blaby LA; Corby LA; Daventry LA; East Northamptonshire LA; Kettering LA; Northampton LA; South Northamptonshire LA; Wellingborough LA.	Corby; Daventry; Kettering; Northampton North; Northampton South; Leicestershire South; Northamptonshire South; Wellingborough
48	Nottingham & Leicestershire North West	Charnwood LA; Gedling LA; Hinckley and Bosworth LA; North West Leicestershire LA; Nottingham UA; Rushcliffe LA.	Bosworth; Gedling; Loughborough; Leicestershire North West; Nottingham East; Nottingham North; Nottingham South; Rushcliffe
49	Nottinghamshire North & Chesterfield	Bassetlaw LA; Bolsover LA; Chesterfield LA; Mansfield LA; Newark and Sherwood LA; North East Derbyshire LA.	Bassetlaw; Bolsover; Chesterfield; Mansfield; Newark; Derbyshire North East; Sherwood
50	Peak District	Amber Valley LA; Ashfield LA; Broxtowe LA; Derbyshire Dales LA; Erewash LA; High Peak LA; Staffordshire Moorlands LA.	Amber Valley; Ashfield; Broxtowe; Derbyshire Dales; Erewash; High Peak; Derbyshire Mid; Staffordshire Moorlands

(Continued)

(Continued)

Area #	European Constituency	2001 Local Authorities	2010 Westminster Constituencies
North West			
51	Cheshire East	Halton UA; Macclesfield LA; Vale Royal LA; Warrington UA.	Altrincham & Sale West; Halton; Macclesfield; Tatton; Warrington North; Warrington South; Weaver Vale
52	Cheshire West & Wirral	Chester LA; Crewe and Nantwich LA; Ellesmere Port and Neston LA; Wirral MB.	Birkenhead; Chester, City of; Crewe & Nantwich; Eddisbury; Ellesmere Port & Neston; Wallasey; Wirral South; Wirral West
53	Cumbria & Lancashire North	Allerdale LA; Barrow-in-Furness LA; Carlisle LA; Copeland LA; Eden LA; Lancaster LA; South Lakeland LA; Wyre LA.	Barrow & Furness; Carlisle; Copeland; Lancaster & Fleetwood; Morecambe & Lunesdale; Penrith & The Border; Westmorland & Lonsdale; Workington
54	Greater Manchester Central	Manchester MB; Stockport MB.	Blackley & Broughton; Cheadle; Hazel Grove; Manchester Central; Manchester Gorton; Manchester Withington; Stockport; Wythenshawe & Sale East
55	Greater Manchester East	Oldham MB; Rochdale MB; Tameside MB.	Ashton Under Lyne; Denton & Reddish; Heywood & Middleton; Oldham East & Saddleworth; Oldham West & Royton; Rochdale; Stalybridge & Hyde
56	Greater Manchester West	Bolton MB; Salford MB; Trafford MB.	Bolton North East; Bolton South East; Bolton West; Bury South; Salford & Eccles; Stretford & Urmston; Worsley & Eccles South
57	Lancashire Central	Blackpool UA; Burnley LA; Fylde LA; Pendle LA; Preston LA; Ribble Valley LA.	Blackpool North & Cleveleys; Blackpool South; Burnley; Fylde; Pendle; Preston; Ribble Valley; Wyre & Preston North
58	Lancashire South	Blackburn with Darwen UA; Bury MB; Chorley LA; Hyndburn LA; Rossendale LA; South Ribble LA; West Lancashire LA.	Blackburn; Bury North; Chorley; Hyndburn; Rossendale & Darwen; South Ribble; Lancashire West
59	Merseyside East & Wigan	Knowsley MB; St Helens MB; Wigan MB.	Knowsley; Leigh; Makerfield; St Helens North; St Helens South & Whiston; Wigan

Area #	European Constituency	2001 Local Authorities	2010 Westminster Constituencies
60	Merseyside West	Liverpool MB; Sefton MB.	Bootle; Garston & Halewood; Liverpool Riverside; Liverpool Walton; Liverpool Wavertree; Liverpool West Derby; Sefton Central; Southport
Yorkshire and the Humber				

Area #	European Constituency	2001 Local Authorities	2010 Westminster Constituencies
61	East Yorkshire & North Lincolnshire	East Riding of Yorkshire UA; Kingston upon Hull, City of UA; North Lincolnshire UA.	Beverley & Holderness; Brigg & Goole; Yorkshire East; Haltemprice & Howden; Hull East; Hull North; Hull West & Hessle; Scunthorpe
62	Leeds	Leeds MB.	Elmet & Rothwell; Leeds Central; Leeds East; Leeds North East; Leeds North West; Leeds West; Morley & Outwood; Pudsey
63	North Yorkshire	Craven LA; Harrogate LA; Ryedale LA; Scarborough LA; Selby LA; York UA.	Harrogate & Knaresborough; Scarborough & Whitby; Selby & Ainsty; Skipton & Ripon; Thirsk & Malton; York Central; York Outer
64	Sheffield	Sheffield MB.	Penistone & Stocksbridge; Sheffield Central; Sheffield South East; Sheffield Brightside & Hillsborough; Sheffield Hallam; Sheffield Heeley
65	Yorkshire South	Barnsley MB; Doncaster MB; Rotherham MB.	Barnsley Central; Barnsley East; Don Valley; Doncaster Central; Doncaster North; Rother Valley; Rotherham; Wentworth & Dearne
66	Yorkshire South West	Kirklees MB; Wakefield MB.	Batley & Spen; Colne Valley; Dewsbury; Hemsworth; Huddersfield; Normanton, Pontefract & Castleford; Wakefield
67	Yorkshire West	Bradford MB; Calderdale MB.	Bradford East; Bradford South; Bradford West; Calder Valley; Halifax; Keighley; Shipley

North East

Area #	European Constituency	2001 Local Authorities	2010 Westminster Constituencies
68	Cleveland & Richmond	Hambleton LA; Hartlepool UA; Middlesborough UA; Redcar and Cleveland UA; Richmondshire LA; Stockton-on-Tees UA.	Hartlepool; Middlesbrough; Middlesbrough South & Cleveland; Redcar; Richmond (Yorks); Stockton North; Stockton South

(Continued)

(Continued)

Area #	European Constituency	2001 Local Authorities	2010 Westminster Constituencies
69	Durham	Chester-le-Street LA; Darlington UA; Derwentside LA; Durham LA; Easington LA; Sedgefield LA; Teesdale LA; Wear Valley LA.	Bishop Auckland; Blaydon; Durham, City of; Darlington; Easington; Durham North; Durham North West; Sedgefield
70	Northumbria	Alnwick LA; Berwick-upon-Tweed LA; Blyth Valley LA; Castle Morpeth LA; Newcastle upon Tyne MB; North Tyneside MB; Tynedale LA; Wansbeck LA.	Berwick-upon-Tweed; Blyth Valley; Hexham; Newcastle upon Tyne Central; Newcastle upon Tyne North; Tyneside North; Tynemouth; Wansbeck
71	Tyne & Wear	Gateshead MB; South Tyneside MB; Sunderland MB.	Gateshead; Houghton & Sunderland South; Jarrow; Newcastle upon Tyne East; South Shields; Sunderland Central; Washington & Sunderland West
		Wales	
72	Mid & West Wales	Carmarthenshire UA; Ceredigion UA; Pembrokeshire UA; Powys UA.	Brecon & Radnorshire; Carmarthen East & Dinefwr; Carmarthen West & Pembrokeshire; Ceredigion; Dwyfor Meirionnydd; Llanelli; Montgomeryshire; Preseli Pembrokeshire
73	North Wales	Conwy UA; Denbighshire UA; Flintshire UA; Gwynedd UA; Isle of Anglesey UA; Wrexham UA.	Aberconwy; Alyn & Deeside; Arfon; Clwyd South; Clwyd West; Delyn; Vale of Clwyd; Wrexham; Ynys Mon
74	South Wales Central	Cardiff UA; Rhondda, Cynon, Taff UA; Vale of Glamorgan, The UA.	Cardiff Central; Cardiff North; Cardiff South & Penarth; Cardiff West; Cynon Valley; Pontypridd; Rhondda; Vale of Glamorgan
75	South Wales East	Blaenau Gwent UA; Caerphilly UA; Merthyr Tydfil UA; Monmouthshire UA; Newport UA; Torfaen UA.	Blaenau Gwent; Caerphilly; Islwyn; Merthyr Tydfil & Rhymney; Monmouth; Newport East; Newport West; Torfaen

Area #	European Constituency	2001 Local Authorities	2010 Westminster Constituencies
76	South Wales West	Bridgend UA; Neath Port Talbot UA; Swansea UA.	Aberavon; Bridgend; Gower; Neath; Ogmore; Swansea East; Swansea West
Scotland			
77	Central Scotland	East Ayrshire CA; Falkirk CA; North Lanarkshire CA; South Lanarkshire CA.	Airdrie & Shotts; Coatbridge, Chryston & Bellshill; Cumbernauld, Kilsyth & Kirkintilloch; East Kilbride, Strathaven & Lesmahagow; Falkirk; Kilmarnock & Loudoun; Lanark & Hamilton East; Motherwell & Wishaw; Rutherglen & Hamilton West
78	Glasgow	Glasgow City CA.	Glasgow Central; Glasgow East; Glasgow North; Glasgow North East; Glasgow North West; Glasgow South; Glasgow South West; Argyll & Bute
79	Highlands & Islands	Argyll and Bute CA; Eilean Siar CA; Highland CA; Moray CA; Orkney Islands CA; Shetland Islands CA.	Caithness, Sutherland & Easter Ross; Inverness, Nairn, Badenoch & Strathspey; Moray; Na h-Eileanan an Iar (Western Isles); Orkney & Shetland; Ross, Skye & Lochaber
80	Lothian	Edinburgh, City of CA; Midlothian CA; West Lothian CA.	Edinburgh East; Edinburgh North & Leith; Edinburgh South; Edinburgh South West; Edinburgh West; Linlithgow & Falkirk East; Livingston; Midlothian
81	Mid Scotland & Fife	Clackmannanshire CA; Fife CA; Perth and Kinross CA; Stirling CA.	Dunfermline & Fife West; Glenrothes; Kirkcaldy & Cowdenbeath; Fife North East; Ochil & South Perthshire; Perth & North Perthshire; Stirling
82	North East Scotland	Aberdeen City CA; Aberdeenshire CA; Angus CA; Dundee City CA.	Aberdeen North; Aberdeen South; Angus; Banff & Buchan; Dundee East; Dundee West; Gordon; Aberdeenshire West & Kincardine
83	South of Scotland	Dumfries and Galloway CA; East Lothian CA; North Ayrshire CA; Scottish Borders, The CA; South Ayrshire CA.	Ayr, Carrick & Cumnock; Berwickshire, Roxburgh & Selkirk; Ayrshire Central; Dumfries & Galloway; Dumfriesshire, Clydesdale & Tweedale; East Lothian

(Continued)

(Continued)

Area #	European Constituency	2001 Local Authorities	2010 Westminster Constituencies
84	West of Scotland	East Dunbartonshire CA; East Renfrewshire CA; Inverclyde CA; Renfrewshire CA; West Dunbartonshire CA.	Dunbartonshire East; Renfrewshire East; Inverclyde; Ayrshire North & Arran; Paisley & Renfrewshire North; Paisley & Renfrewshire South; Dunbartonshire West
Northern Ireland			
85	Northern Ireland	All in Northern Ireland	All in Northern Ireland

Note: LA = local authority, LB = London borough, UA = unitary authority, MB = metropolitan borough, CA = council area

Brief reference list

This book was written for students at university studying at the start of the twenty-first century, assumed to be living in, or interested in, the UK. Given this audience, it was assumed that they would all be computer literate and could search for sources or further information on the World Wide Web. That is why almost all the further reading at the end of each chapter is in sources to be found on the Web. It was also assumed that they would not welcome the insertion in this text of numerous references to printed works, many of which could only be found in a few university libraries. The other main sources that were used in writing this book and drawing the maps shown here were:

The population censuses of 1981, 1991 and 2001 (http://cdu.mimas.ac.uk/lct/)
Social Trends (www.statistics.gov.uk)
The House of Commons Library web pages (in particular for the definitions of the areas mapped: www.parliament.uk/documents/commons/lib/research/rp98/rp98–102.pdf)
The neighbourhood statistics website of the Office for National Statistics (www.neighbourhood.statistics.gov.uk/dissemination/)
The General Register Office for Scotland website (www.gro-scotland.gov.uk)
Results published from the Youth Cohort Study of England and Wales (www.education.gov.uk/rsgateway/DB/SFR/s000560/index.shtml)
Publications of the Higher Education Council for England (in particular www.hefce.ac.uk/pubs/hefce/2001/01_62.htm)
Seymour, J. (ed.), 2001, *Poverty in Plenty: A Human Development Report for the UK*, Earthscan Publications Ltd, London, ISBN 1 85383 707 5 (http://booklens.com/jane-seymour/poverty-in-plenty)
Work on worldwide trends published by The Townsend Centre for International Poverty Research at the University of Bristol (www.bris.ac.uk/poverty) in association with UNICEF (www.bristol.ac.uk/poverty/press%20and%20consultation_files/child%20poverty.html): Gordon, D., et al., 'The Distribution of Child Poverty in the Developing World: Report to UNICEF', Centre for International Poverty Research, University of Bristol, Bristol, 2003.

For further information type 'human geography of the UK' into your search engine. At the time of writing, over one million web pages were linked to this phrase, ordered roughly by relevance to the subject. Don't be put off by how much is written about the UK – it remains a small island!

Index